The Master's Cowboy:

An Autobiography

The Master's Cowboy:

An Autobiography

Arless Glass

The Master's Cowboy:
An Autobiography

By Arless Glass

Cover design by Laura Merchant, interior layout Tim Cummings

Printed in United States of America
Published by

WORD AFLAME PRESS
8855 Dunn Road, Hazelwood, MO 63042
www.pentecostalpublishing.com

Library of Congress Cataloging-in-Publication Data

Glass, Arless, 1929-
   The master's cowboy : an autobiography / by Arless Glass.
      p. cm.
   ISBN 978-0-7577-4355-9
1. Glass, Arless, 1929- 2. Pentecostals--United States--Biography. 3. Pentecostal churches--Texas--Pasadena--Clergy--Biography. I. Title.
   BX8762.Z8G53 2012
   289.9'4092--dc23
   [B]
                                        2012029848

Dedication

Jesus Christ is to be praised and thanked for giving me such an exciting life and for saving me from the many blunders and mistakes I have made. I am totally nothing without Him! This book is dedicated to my children and stepchildren, my many friends, and my church family who strongly encourged me to put forth my life in writing.

A very special dedication to Claude and Mary Sirmons for editing and helping me in the arrangements of the contents. I owe so much to so many.

"COWBOY"

When I was a little boy,
Just a kid and all,
Big as anyone, I thought,
Though mostly I was small;

I spent a lot of good ol' days
On my daddy's knee
Or riding on the stick-horse limb
That I cut down from a tree.

With my trusty gun of make-believe
Strapped down on my side,
I'd mount up on that leafless branch,
And away I would ride.

I'd chase out all the bad guys,
And other varmint pests.
When it came to Injun fighter,
I was just about the best.

I was never known to be out-drawed,
And my stick never tired.
Pity the wretched outlaw
That strayed into my yard.
Folks gave me a nickname,
And I'm afraid it came to stay.
I guess I'm known as "Cowboy"
Until this very day.

Way out west of the back porch steps
I spent many a day

Doing good and fighting bad,
But then it was only play.

Little boys with make-believe toys
Make the world a better place
For a kind old dad with a heart full of love
And a smile upon his face.

But childhood dreams and childish things
Must sadly see an end;
Then loving dads, just a little sad,
See their baby boys as men.

The years have come to me and gone,
And I think I can safely say
That I've done my best and done some good
Without wasting many days.

I've traded weapons of make-believe
For another kind of sword,
And now I chase the bad guys
For the glory of the Lord.

I think I've made some friends along
As I've followed God's own way.
And one of those is the very one
Who wrote these words today.

When you need a thoughtful friend
To make your bad guys flee,
Just call for the Master's "cowboy";
Praise the Lord, that's me.

Roger Russell

Table of Contents

THE FAMILY

John Ohma Glass gave me my name, Arless. Where he came up with that name I don't know. It means "a penny, a king, a pledge." While visiting Germany in 1982 I saw a street sign reading "Arless," but otherwise it is not a name I often see. My mother's maiden name was Richey, so I was born Arless Richey Glass, August 17, 1929, to Robert Newton and Elmira Elnora (Allie) Richey Glass.

I was born one month early by caesarean, due to the health of my mother, in Frazier Clinic in DeRidder, Louisiana. The medical staff gave me no chance to live, so the nurse put me in a dresser drawer in the room and left me. They were working feverishly with my mother because they were afraid she would die. A neighbor came in during this time to visit Mother—Mrs. Lola Barnhill, who was a good Baptist neighbor. The nurses were still tending my mother when Mrs. Barnhill interrupted and asked, "Where is the baby?" She was told that the baby was in the dresser drawer and that he was dying or already dead.

She opened the drawer, saw that I was breathing, handed me to the nurse, and said, "Clean him up! He is going to live! God has a work for him to do!"

Against the nurse's better judgment and the doctor's orders, she took me and cleaned me. Much to their surprise, I lived.

After Mother was discharged from the hospital, Mrs. Barnhill was a faithful visitor and helper, and she assisted Mother through her healing process. Not long after that, Mother converted her, and she became a Pentecostal and a lifelong friend of the Glass family. She had a son named Larry, who, after coming home from the Navy in 1946, married my sister, Lucille.

I suppose I should tell a little more about my ancestry. The Glass family emigrated from Germany (Saxony) to England, then to the United States. They came in the late 1600s and settled in Virginia. The name was spelled Glafs, but they changed it to Glass. On the Glass coat of arms is the motto, "I struggle but am not overwhelmed." I traced the family history back to 1742, when a grandfather was born. From Virginia, some Glasses moved to Merewether County, Georgia. Then a part of the family moved to Marthaville, Louisiana.

In tracing the genealogy of the Glass family, I found dad's father, John, with only four children, and I knew he had six. Finally I found the answer. His first wife, Isabella, died and he married her twin sister, Isabel. He and Isabel had twin daughters. John moved further south to Beauregard Parish, which at the time was a huge cotton-producing area. There he started the first cotton gin in Louisiana and also established the first Masonic lodge in that part of the country. It is still active in Magnolia, Louisiana, and my grandfather's grave is there, five miles from Bear.

My mother was the most amazing lady I have ever known. She was born on May 8, 1889, to Daniel and Elizabeth Richey in Bear, Louisiana, a town later renamed Ragley. I know very little about her family history and must have been sixty years old before I knew any of it. I know the Richey family emigrated from England to the United States in the early 1800s. They landed in Galveston and soon moved to Houston. Richey Streets in Pasadena and Houston are probably named after them. From Houston, two brothers started to Oklahoma and one to Louisiana.

On the way to Oklahoma, they encountered the forced march of the Cherokee Indians, along the "trail of tears." Daniel Richey's father somehow managed to kidnap his bride from the Indians. She was a princess, the daughter of an Indian chief. To escape from the authorities, they headed to Louisiana, where he knew he could conceal the fact that she was an Indian from Oklahoma because many Acadian families lived there. These people are descendants of the French people expelled from what is now the Maritime provinces of Canada in the 1700s and are usually dark skinned. Her complexion was similar, and they could pass her off as "Cajun." At that time, to proud Southern families, it was a disgrace to be married to an Indian; therefore, it was never discussed. We were always told that she was of French descent. We have no documents to prove this as they did not record it. I'm sure I was present when my mother and two of her sisters talked for hours, mentioning dates and places, but I was too young or uninterested to pay attention. Now I'm sorry that I didn't listen or ask questions. I sometimes wondered about the high cheekbones of my mother and me. They speak of Indian blood, and I'm proud of that now. If I had known my heritage as a late teenager, it would have meant a free college education. My mother's sister, the mother of my cousin Carman Richey Havens, was a journalist in the late 1800s and early 1900s. My brother Bill talked to her, and she told him much about this part of the Richey family history.

In 1910, my mother married Glenn McCorqudale, and their son, Glendon was born in 1911. Shortly after the birth of his son, Glenn left home, and mother heard that he went to California. He was proven unfaithful to Mother, and the marriage ended in divorce.

Mother's family were "shouting Methodists," but as time went on the Methodists stopped shouting and began aligning with other denominations, not believing in the power of God or the demonstration of the Spirit.

Mother's family was heartbroken and disappointed over this. Mother was in DeQuincy, Louisiana, in 1914 when she happened to see a brush arbor (a frame built with leafy limbs or tall brush placed on top to provide shade). She heard the people singing and was curious about what was going on, so she went over, walked in, and sat on a crude bench. The preacher began preaching and explaining how God was pouring out His Spirit. He stated that everybody needs the baptism of the Holy Ghost with the evidence of speaking in tongues as the Spirit gives the utterance, according to Acts 2:4. She listened, and when the preacher gave an altar call, Mother went to the front. She received the Holy Ghost with the evidence of speaking in tongues there.

When she went home, she told her mother and sisters, "I have found old-fashioned Methodism." She explained the service to them, that the preacher said she needed the Holy Ghost evidenced by speaking with tongues, and that she received that experience. As soon as they could, they went to DeQuincy, and her mother and two sisters soon received the Holy Ghost, too.

After a few weeks, Mother heard that one of her cousins, Benny Baggett, had received this experience and was preaching revivals wherever he could. She contacted him and began to travel with him and his wife in evangelistic work. She was the song leader, special singer, altar worker, and also the washer-woman. In November 1915 after service was over, Mother was sitting on a front bench when Brother Baggett sat beside her and said, "Sister Allie, there's a new doctrine going around."

"What is it?" she asked.

"They claim that Jesus is God, and we must be baptized in Jesus' name."

"Brother Benny, what are we going to do?"

"Do? We are going to obey it if it is true. We're going to a conference at Elton next month to discuss it."

At the Elton Bible conference, Mother was special singer and song leader. The ministry discussed all aspects of who Jesus was and how they should baptize. They concluded that, according to Scripture, Jesus is the mighty God and we must be baptized in Jesus' name. They had their first baptismal service on Saturday, December 19, 1915. It was very cold that day, yet they walked a quarter-mile to the river. Mother was the first lady to be baptized, and Brother Oliver Fauss was the first man baptized. Mother said she walked back to the building in freezing weather in wet clothes and didn't even sneeze. They left the conference, and Mother went home and said to her family, "We've been baptized wrong. We must be baptized in the name of Jesus Christ!" Her mother spoke up, "Why, that young whippersnapper! He's trying to steal all the glory from His Father!" Mother then began to explain that there is no Trinity but Jesus is God. She quoted I Timothy 3:16 to them, "Without controversy great is the mystery of godliness: God was manifest in the flesh, justified in the Spirit, seen of angels, preached unto the Gentiles, believed on in the world, received up into glory." She then stated, "That's speaking of Jesus." Her mother said, "Why, I see that." By her simple explanation they all accepted it and were baptized in Jesus' name.

Mother introduced Brother Oliver Fauss to the lady who later became his wife. When they were married, Mother started traveling with them. Brother Fauss wrote the book of his early experiences, *What God Hath Wrought*, and told me that Mother was with him throughout the period the book covered. I have a letter she wrote home in February 1916, which stated, "We have been here in Oakdale for two weeks and only sixteen have received the Holy Ghost. Please pray that we will have a breakthrough."

I don't know when or where my mother and father met. I know he lived about ten miles from her in a community called Fulton. She told him that she would not marry him until he was filled with the Holy Ghost. He was a "good Baptist" and resisted for a while. The night came when he received the Holy Ghost and was baptized in Jesus' name. The next day, a funny thing happened. He went to his job where he used oxen to pull logs out of the woods. He yoked the oxen and tried to get them to move, but they wouldn't. They were so used to hearing him yelling and cursing that they didn't recognize his voice. He tried for quite a while but finally gave up and called someone else to come to work his oxen. Later, Dad was the first man in that area to use trucks to haul timber.

Mother and Dad were married in 1917, and that ended her evangelism traveling as she then had four children to take care of, her own and Dad's three. They said that people would ride for miles to visit Mother to hear her sing for them. (She was a marvelous singer. I would like to say the gift passed to her son, but you wouldn't know which son. I guess the talent jumped a generation to her grandsons. George Junior and Rich just can't be beaten.) She would testify and sing to those who came to hear her, and many of them were filled with the Holy Ghost in the living room. My parents always had a room for every preacher who came through their community. Mother was a charter member of the Bear Pentecostal Church, and when they moved to DeRidder in 1925, she became a member of the Pentecostal church in DeRidder.

I was one of eleven children. My father had been married before and had three children—Blanche, George Lafitte, and John Ohma. His wife died in childbirth with her fourth child, who also died. My mother had also been married before, with one child, Glendon. When Dad and Mother married, they already had a large family, but not the twelve children Dad always said he wanted. These two families merged as one and actually resented calling anyone "stepchild." They had seven more children—Glydus, Robert Orland, William Prentiss (Bill), Medford Leroy, Lucille Elizabeth, Arless Richey, and Charles Earl. Medford, when just a small boy, had heard the term "stepchild," and one day he asked, "Mother, am I your stepchild?" Mother answered, "No. Why do you ask?" He replied, "Well, I can climb a stepladder."

With eleven children to take care of, it was impossible for Mother to take care of all of them, so the older children were assigned someone to care for. Ohma and Glydus were assigned Arless and Charles, and we were their responsibility after they came home from work. Years later, Glydus married and had three children. When she had her fourth one, a boy, her husband called and said, "Glydus wants to name him Arless. Is that all right with you?" Then two years later she had another son, and they called Charles and asked if they could name him Charles. What is amazing is that Arless Lewis looked much like me and Charles Lewis looked a lot like Charles. I know of ten people who have been named after me since then.

Dad had steel-gray eyes that seemed to look right through a person. I would sit around and listen to his stories that sounded good, though I really didn't believe some of them. Then one of his old friends would visit and would tell the same story Dad had told us. I was surprised to learn that he had been a deputy sheriff from 1905 to 1910, and it was amazing to hear some of his experiences. He didn't tell this story, but one of his friends did.

"There was a certain criminal in town guilty of a crime, and your dad was sent to arrest him. He was in a saloon with a number of people and made the boast that when Glass came to get him, he would kill him. A short while later, your dad walked in, walked up to the man who was standing at the bar, took his gun, and ordered him to walk to the jail, which he did. Some of his friends asked him a few days later why he didn't shoot him. He answered, 'When I looked into that man's eyes, I froze. I couldn't do a thing!'"

A few years later, Dad backslid and began drinking heavily and gambling. He lost all his wealth before the Wall Street crash. When the crash came, there was no way he could get financing to continue his company. He quickly quit his drinking and became a family man. He never touched liquor again from my birth on. He was an outstanding husband and father and became one of the most beloved and influential men of the city. We never left home without going to Dad, kissing him on the cheek, and saying good-bye and never came home without kissing him and saying hello. While I was overseas, Geri, my fiancée, had to visit him every day, kiss him on his cheek, and give him a hug. Geri and her mom and dad were adopted into our family and were expected to attend every function of the Glass family.

I never heard my dad criticize one person. I was critical of someone and expressed it to him. He was silent for a moment and said, "Son, if you knew the complete story you might not be so critical. Let me tell you something. When you hear something bad about someone, believe nothing unless you know the whole story. Believe nothing you hear and only half of what you see because your eyes can play tricks on you, too."

He then told me a story about an experience he had while he was deputy sheriff. "A man came riding his horse into town after having ridden all day. He went to the hotel, went in, paid for a room, and then took his horse to the livery stable. He went back to his room and was so tired he fell across the bed with his clothes and boots on. He lay there a few minutes when he heard a scream from down the hall. He jumped to his feet and ran down the hall to an open door, where he heard gasping coming from the room. He rushed in and saw a man climbing out the window; at the same time he saw a man with a knife in his chest falling backward. He wanted to help but didn't know what to do, so he grabbed the knife and yanked it out of the man's chest. As he did, four people rushed to the door. They saw him with the bloodied knife, holding it in the position as if he was going to stab the man again.

"When the law came, the man surrendered the knife and tried to explain what happened. The four witnesses said they saw the man plunge the knife into the victim and was about to plunge it in again. We had his trial in the next few days. He declared his innocence, but no one would believe him. At his trial the four people testified they had seen him plunge the knife into the victim and was about to plunge it in again. The jury heard this testimony, and only the man could deny it. They found him guilty and sentenced him to death by hanging in two weeks. The two weeks came, the scaffold was built, and the man was hanged. The next day a man came into the sheriff's office and screamed to us that we had hanged an innocent man! He said he was the guilty man and that he could not live with himself seeing another man die for a murder that he had committed." Dad stated again, "Believe nothing you hear and only half of what you see." I understood why Dad would never criticize a person.

I wish I could write about my first year, but I don't remember it. I am sure it was a very exciting year. I did hit the world with such impact that the blow brought on the Great Depression! I was so excited to be alive that I couldn't speak for at least a year and then could only say a few words. I was a very sickly child. After I learned to walk, I came down with a disease then called "blood flux," an unnatural discharge of blood or liquid matter from the body, and I was given up to die. Mother stayed beside me night and day, praying continually. God heard her prayers and healed me. I had to learn to walk again. Then, a few months later, I came down with double pneumonia and was again given up to die. In those days pneumonia was fatal. So again, my faithful mother stayed with me night and day. One evening the family persuaded her to leave me for a few hours to get some rest. Finally, she decided that it would be good to rest awhile. She started to leave; I opened my eyes and said, "Goodbye." That scared her so badly that she sat by the bed and would not leave me at all. What a mother! I survived that and had to learn to walk all over again. Some say, "Three strikes and you're out!" But it certainly was not true with me! Maybe that was God strengthening my body against many diseases, as I have been very healthy for the rest of my life.

Mother could quote her alphabet forward and backward, so she taught me to do the same by the time I was four. That made me feel proud, but the first few weeks of school were surely boring while the other students were learning their ABCs.

I never liked my name, Arless, but it was all right until I got into high school, where the other teenagers called me many variations of it. I would complain about it but, of course, could do nothing about it. I even received a letter while in high school from the Texas State College of Women asking me to enroll, and I thought it was disgraceful.

The Glass Family
Left to right standing: John Ohma, George, William (Bill), Medford, me, Charles, Glendon, Robert Orland.
Front row: Blanche, mother, Glydus, Lucille, dad.

It is strange that I was the only one of eleven in the Glass family born in a hospital, yet the only one without a birth certificate.

They were so sure I wouldn't make it that they didn't even record my birth. When I enlisted in the air force in 1950, I needed a birth certificate. My father was the health inspector of Beauregard Parish, so I went to his head nurse to have her assist me in getting one. Instead, she typed me one right there in her office. Years later, having misplaced that certificate, I applied to the state for one and found that none existed. The hospital had no record of my birth. I had to go to my oldest sister, Blanche Alston, and to a number of people in the city who had known me all my life to have them attest to the fact that I had been born. Strangely, they couldn't tell by looking; I had to have them verify the fact that I existed. If I had applied to the state, it would have been at least six months before I could have gotten it. The Lord wanted me in the air force at His time.

Dr. Frazier was not only our family doctor but also a longtime friend of my father. He and my father went to medical college together. My father quit medical college six months before graduation. The instructors had brought a nine-year-old orphan girl in to dissect. Dad took one look at her and said to the other students, "Let's bury her, boys." They did, and my father walked out and wouldn't complete college.

Dr. Frazier, at my birth, put his finger in Dad's face and said, "Bob, don't you dare have another child! Allie will not be able to live through it!" Dad listened for a couple of years. Then, since Mother's health had improved, he wanted another child. He had his heart set on twelve children! Charles was born on Mother's Day and Mother's birthday, May 8, 1932. His name was to be Charles Aaron, but somehow the one writing the birth certificate made a mistake and wrote, "Charles Earl." This time Dr. Frazier was more forceful than ever. "Allie can't have another child! She will die. She has a large tumor in her body, and another child will kill her!" Mother was then forty-three years old. Through time, God healed her of the tumor, and she was healthy until she had a stroke at eighty years of age. She was placed in a nursing home, where she lived another two years. What a mother! Her strong faith is with us today! Near the end she could barely talk or lift her head from the pillow, but when asked the question, "Mother, what is the plan of salvation?" she would sit up in bed and say very strongly, "Then Peter said unto them, Repent, and be baptized every one of you in the name of Jesus Christ for the remission of sins, and ye shall receive the gift of the Holy Ghost." Then she would fall back on her pillow, hardly able to speak. What a mother!

When I was three years old, we lived on Third Street in De-Ridder, having moved from Fulton Street about a year before. I saw a man riding a horse in the alley behind our house. I then made a mistake I would live with the rest of my life. My sister Lucille was taking care of me, and I pointed to the rider and said, "Cowboy! Cowboy! He's not 'Cowboy' any more! I'm Cowboy!" Lucille told that to Dad, and from that day forward I was called "Cowboy." When I was in my late teens, I began to wonder if Dad knew my real name. In church one evening, Brother "Snookie" (a nickname, but I never heard his first name) Alston, our Sunday school teacher, was leading the service, and he wanted to acknowledge my brother Orland and me for some reason. He said, "Brother Ar . . . Ar . . .oh!—Brother Cowboy and Brother Red!" Yes, I have ridden a horse a few times in my life—very few times—but I do have some boots. And I have a horse!

Me and my horse

During the thirties we were in the Great Depression, and money was very scarce. Jobs could not be found and everybody suffered. I say "suffered," but we children really didn't think anything about it. We didn't have a lot of things, but we were happy. My brothers, George and Ohma, worked at the flooring plant for twenty cents an hour. A rumor circulated that a job was available there, and over four hundred men were at the company the next day seeking the rumored job. Dad worked at a gravel company for $4.50 per week. Glydus worked at DeRidder Steam Laundry at ten cents an hour. Because George and Ohma were working at the flooring plant, they were able to furnish us with a house on Third Street. It was a two-bedroom house with a path.

Glendon had left home for California in 1928, a year before I was born. I saw him the first time when he came home for a visit in 1948. He brought his father with him. The older people who knew him gave his father a cold reception. Because of this, Glendon thought the cold reception was for him, and they only stayed three days and left. He determined he would never come back. When I was in Camp Stoneman, I called him a number of times, but he was always too busy to visit me.

Years later, in 1966, I walked into my mother's kitchen and found her crying. I asked her why she was crying, and she answered, "I was thinking of Glendon. I know I will never see him again."

"Mother, you will see him again!" I said.

She didn't believe it, saying that he would never come home again. I then told her I was going to get him home and that we would have a family reunion. That really excited Mother.

When I arrived home in Pasadena, Texas, I called him. He lived in Bakersfield, California. I told him why I was calling and told him we were having a family reunion and wanted him to come home for it. He sounded excited and said he would try to make it. A couple of days later he called me and said he would love to come but couldn't make it. When he said that, I went to a travel agency, purchased him a round-trip ticket to Houston, and sent it to him. I waited three days for him to receive it and called him again. When he recognized my voice he shouted, "I'll be there! I'll be there! Arless, I'll be there!" When he got the ticket in the mail, it made him feel that he was really wanted.

I picked him up at the airport, recognizing him from an old picture I had. We went to DeRidder, where he stayed four days and was thrilled beyond words. Mother was so happy! Many friends heard he was home, and they came from as far as 150 miles to see him. There was a constant flow of people coming in to visit, and to the Glass family it was heaven on earth! Charles was there but his wife, Mary Jo, couldn't travel because of sickness. Charles persuaded him to leave a day early and swing by Sherman to see her. I rode with them to Sherman and then back to Houston for his flight back to Bakersfield. We talked all the way. He made one statement, "Mother's church is the right one, and I won't darken the door of another!"

Charles and I planned to visit him the next year. Before we could visit, he passed away. He appeared to be the picture of health but that silent killer, hypertension, took him out. The doctor said that just a small pill would have saved him, but he would not go to a doctor. Bill, Charles, and I went to the funeral, and Charles and I conducted the service. Mother was in ill health at the time, and we never told her he had passed away. Glendon's wife, JoAnn, would write mother and keep in touch, never mentioning Glendon's death. I still make a fruitcake for Margaret, his daughter, and call her often. I have also visited her and taken her to church with me.

George received the Holy Ghost in 1932 and soon after that was called into the ministry. He had no suit, but Ohma had saved and bought a suit for himself. Ohma was a very handsome man and very popular. He had a photographic memory and could talk on any subject. He kept us spellbound quoting Shakespeare, and we would all flock around him when he was home, begging him to tell us stories. He is the one everyone thought would be called to the ministry. George was rather shy and quiet and talked very little. But God called George to preach, and Ohma was very proud of him. He was his greatest supporter, and he gave George his suit so he would look good for the ministry. George would walk ten miles to a country home and preach on the front porch, where a crowd would gather to hear him. Then he would walk ten miles back that night and would work the next day. He married Clovie Nichols in 1930 and moved to an apartment next door to our church on Mahlon (later changed to Malone) Street. It consisted of one room with a kitchen shared with Brother and Sister Fred Henderson. His son, George Jr., was born there in 1932.

The WPA, Work Projects Administration, was formed by President Roosevelt to help put people to work. Times were very hard. Our nation entered the Great Depression after the stock market crash in 1929. The WPA furnished sewing machines and material for the ladies to make clothing for their families. Mother made all the clothes we younger ones wore. She actually made certain clothes for the entire family. We were a happy family and never thought anything about it, just remained thankful to have something to wear. It wasn't just our family but everyone we knew was in the same situation. We always had food on the table, very little meat but plenty of vegetables because everyone had a garden and shared. We had chickens for eggs and a milk cow. For some reason I never could learn to milk! Mother tried to teach me, but I could never learn. I wonder now if that was not on purpose. Maybe it was because one day I tried to pet the cow and she hooked me. Barely missing my eye, she split my flesh just above it and tore my overalls, too. I was four years old, and from that day I kept my distance from her.

We had no transportation other than our feet. We walked everywhere we went. I can still see my mother walking to church carrying Charles, holding my hand, with Glydus, Lucille, Bill, Orland, and Medford walking along. The church was about a mile away, but we never missed a service. We were taught to be in every service. If we were sick, we went to church for prayer, and God would heal us. Revival was seven nights a week and seldom lasted under two weeks, usually four and five. We never got out of service before ten, but most of the time it was eleven. I have taken many naps under the benches with people shouting all around me.

The Barnhills lived across the street from us until they moved to another house in 1934. One day I was playing on the porch of the empty house they had vacated, jumping from the porch to the ground, when I spied a penny! I picked it up and ran to the house shouting, "I found a penny!" The whole neighborhood knew about it. That was a lot of money! The school was a half block away, and the next day Lucille, at noon break, came to me with her girlfriend and asked to borrow that penny. I was so disappointed, and I didn't want to give it to her. I felt rich carrying that penny in my pocket, but she was with her girlfriend and I didn't want to embarrass her. I reached way down in my pocket (it seemed my pocket reached to my knees), took hold of that penny, and gave it to her. She never did pay me back! When the First Pentecostal Church in DeRidder had a service honoring her on her eightieth birthday, Brother Zale Lewis invited me to speak. I reminded Lucille that I had one thing against her— that penny! She spoke up, "I'll pay you back!" I answered, "Yes, seventy-five years later! There is no way that penny could ever be paid back, but being the big-hearted brother that I am, I forgive you."

Brother Luther Nichols, who later entered the ministry, moved his family into the house previously occupied by the Barnhills. His son, James Dale, and I were already friends but became like brothers. We had a friendship that lasted over seventy years until his death. Today I am privileged to know his son, Scott. He is James Dale all over again to me. I use his name James Dale, for he said years later, "There are a lot of James Nicholses, but there is only one James Dale Nichols." I was quick to agree with him.

I started school at the age of six; that first day I felt grown up. I walked to school with a big grin on my face and heard the neighbors say to me, "You're going to school! My, how big you are!" I believe my grin became wider. Now I wonder why they seemed so glad. I thought I was a little angel, but what I have heard in later years makes me doubt that.

When I entered the building, I got scared! I don't know why. The picture is forever etched in my mind of sitting with my elbow on the desk and my chin in my hand, afraid to look up. When they had recess, I got out of there! I ran home. Unfortunately for me, Dad was at home. He took a belt and whipped me all the way back to school! I'm sorry there was not a policeman on the schoolyard! He could have arrested my dad for child abuse!

No! No! Come to think of it, that was the rule of the day. The teachers were allowed to spank the children, and they took advantage of it! I know they say today that it will "warp the child's personality." Well, our personalities were warped quite a few times back then. According to today's thinking, our generation and those before us didn't have a chance! Parents had no qualms about spanking their children; they just did it! Did I resent my dad for such abuse? Absolutely not! He was the greatest dad in the world! There was never a question about Dad loving his children. I was one who believed that of eleven children, he loved me best of all! He was firm in his teachings and discipline, and all of his children loved him for it. We are thankful today for the way he and Mother raised us! I was glad the classes were in session that day, though, because I went back to class and no one knew about the punishment I received. School let out at noon the first day. When I got home, Dad thought I had left again and was preparing to send me back when Lucille came to my rescue and told Dad there was no school that afternoon. She barely saved me from another spanking. The next day and from then on, I was all right.

All my life I believed that I was Dad's favorite. He loved me most of all! Twenty-five years after my father's death, I was talking to my brother Bill. (Bill moved to Pasadena in 1962, just after I became pastor of the United Pentecostal Church of Pasadena, and remained with me until his death in 2004. His wife, Molly, is still with me. It was such a delight to pastor my brother. He and Molly received the Holy Ghost in the revival we conducted in DeRidder in 1954. He strongly supported me all those years.) Bill said to me, "Arless, you know, of all of our family, Dad loved me most of all!" I was shocked to hear him say that! I did not answer; I just turned and walked away. I thought, *He knows I was Dad's favorite! Why did he say that?* A few weeks later George came to visit. I knew George believed that I was Dad's favorite, so I said to him in Bill's presence, "George, Bill told me a few weeks ago that he was Dad's favorite!" I was ready for George to refute that and explain to him that I was, when he said, "That's not true, Bill. I was Dad's favorite!" Then I learned that Dad had a way of making every one of his children believe he was his favorite. Months later a cousin, Marvin Cooley, came to visit Bill. They were talking about Dad, when Marvin said, "You know, Bill, Uncle Bob loved me more than any child he had!" What a man! What a dad! I feel I have inherited that from him. Every person I meet is very important to me!

One day my sister, Blanche Alston, who lived in DeQuincy, Louisiana, came to see us. She brought two pairs of boots. She said she had bought them for her daughters, Juanita, who was the age of Lucille, and Betty June, who was one year younger than me. They could not wear them, so she said, "Maybe Arless and Charles can wear them." Her husband, Des, had a good job and she knew Dad could not afford such for us, so this was her excuse. Her son, who was one year older than me, had died the year before. They were the most beautiful boots in the world, and they fit me perfectly! I was anxious to wear them to school the next day.

The next morning it was cold. Our neighbor, Bobby Hinton, came to the house to eat breakfast with us, and then we were going to walk to school together. There was one problem, he was barefoot. His father had been killed in an automobile accident two years before, and Bobby, no doubt, didn't have any shoes. As we were getting ready to leave, my mother looked at me and said, "Son, Bobby doesn't have any shoes." I had my boots in my hand to put on, looked at them, then very slowly handed them to Bobby. So I never got to wear those boots! Someone said later how selfless and noble of me to do that. I stated, "No, I deserve no praise for that! I didn't want to. I didn't do it because I wanted to. He just needed some shoes, and I had another pair. So, no, I should get no praise for doing something I didn't want to do." I will say, however, that I coveted those boots for a while, especially when he would remove them to run on the playground and I would see them. I would say in my mind, *My boots!* The next pair of boots I received was given to me by the United Pentecostal Church of Pasadena in 1965. Since then, boots have been a big part of my life.

Then, wonder of wonders, my father's nephew, A. J. Lambert, who had a contract with the Magnolia Oil Company, gave Dad a job driving a dump truck. As a result, we were able to move from Third Street to Warren Street, and there was indoor plumbing! We thought we had finally arrived! We had indoor plumbing, a very large lot, lots of pecan trees (there were no trees on our lot on Third Street), and a garage. We didn't have a car, but the garage made a good playhouse for Charles and me. It was quite a walk to school but worth it! Dad was permitted to use the truck for family, so we would occasionally visit my grandmother and aunts in the country. What a treat! Also, Mother had transportation to church. We lived there for about two years when a friend offered to sell Dad a house for eighteen hundred dollars and to finance it as well. This house was outside the city limits. A couple of hundred yards behind us was a small creek where we could fish and a huge pasture for the cow. That crazy cow would never come home at milking time! Charles and I would have to go deep into the pasture and bring her home every evening. We kept her at the house through the night, and after Mother milked her in the morning, we took her back to the pasture. Finally, Dad sold that cow and purchased another one. Charles said, "It was wonderful when we finally got a cow that had sense enough to come home."

The house had two bedrooms separated from the living room, dining room, and kitchen by a nine-foot hall that went from the front door to the rear wall. There were full-length front and back porches, with part of the back porch taken in for the kitchen. And—it had a path! No water and no electricity, but we had a well, and when we drew water, we always had to strain it because of the "wiggle tails" (mosquito larva). Once we strained it, we used it. We had a number-three washtub we used for our baths, and we took a bath every Saturday whether we needed it or not. We had a big iron pot outside, and we would build a fire under it for Mother on wash day. She would boil the clothes in the wash pot and then rinse them in those washtubs. Our lights consisted of coal-oil lamps. Our only heat was the fireplace, and our wood was pine knots. In winter we covered up with half a dozen quilts on our beds. It was wonderful living! We had nine-foot ceilings, which made the house much cooler in the summer. I must mention our sleeping arrangements. The front bedroom was for Glydus and Lucille. The back bedroom was for Dad, Mother, Medford, Arless, and Charles. The back half of the hall was for Ohma, Bill, and Orland.

In the summer of 1940, Glydus married Fred Lewis, who was a farmer. Glydus came home to have her baby in December of 1941, so Charles and I went to the farm to be with Fred for a few days. When we came home, we walked in, and there on the dining room wall was a switch. I flipped it and a light came on! While we were gone, the REA had installed electricity in our house, and you will never know how wonderful that was to us! Then when Bill came home from World War II, he took his old bedroom—the back half of the hall—and installed a bathroom. Dad then had a butane tank installed and we had gas. I was never so glad to see anything as much as when they put a gas heater in the fireplace! No more chopping pine knots! We were getting "modern" and enclosed part of the front porch for another bedroom. That room was for Charles and me.

Along about then I wanted a gun so badly! I saved my money, and someone had a .22 single-shot rifle, sawed off to be a pistol, which I bought. I was so proud of it! I kept it for a month before it disappeared. I searched everywhere for it, but it could not be found. What happened to that pistol had always been a mystery to me. After I passed seventy-five years of age, Charles asked me about it. I told him it was a mystery to me. Then he said, "Arless, I sold that gun for fifty cents!" Well, at least the mystery was solved.

One morning Dad was driving down a hill with a load of dirt when suddenly some cattle started across the road. There were no stock laws then, and cattle were allowed to roam at will. No way could Dad stop, so he hit one of them and destroyed the truck. There went our transportation, and we were back to walking. We were much farther from the church and the walk was long, but we never missed a service. My brother Ohma saved money for a car and in 1939 bought a 1936 Ford. I remember him driving up to the house, getting out of the car, and walking to the porch, where we were all looking on with amazement. He walked up to Mother and said, "Mother, you will never have to walk to church again!" He was true to his promise.

After the truck was wrecked, in early 1939 Dad leased a service station from A. J., who later sold him a car. The lease price was one cent per gallon of gas sold. My older brothers were working elsewhere, so Dad put me to work at the station even though I was only nine years old. At the time, gas sold for seventeen and one-half cents a gallon, and along with that we aired the tires, cleaned the windshield, and swept the floorboard. Gas wars would happen maybe twice a year, and gas would drop to eleven and one-half cents per gallon. That would last for a few weeks at a time. I would go to school and then to the station, where I would work until six o'clock.

At eleven years of age, I went to the Realart Theater and was given a job popping corn. For the first few weeks the pay was ten cents an hour and then increased to twenty cents. I worked an average of twenty-five hours per week. When I received my paycheck, I always gave Dad half. He did not ask or hint for it. I just felt it was my duty to help along with the others.

As I put this on paper, I cannot believe I did this, but I walked over a mile each morning—Monday through Saturday—opened the station by six, stayed until Dad arrived at 7:45, and drove the car to school. At noon I would drive back to the station so Dad could go to lunch. I would eat a can of potted meat with crackers for my lunch. Then, at 12:50 Dad was back and I drove back to school. When school was over, I went back to the station for an hour, left the car, then on to my job at the theater.

During this time we sold very little gas, and it was extremely rare for someone to say, "Fill 'er up!" Very seldom did someone ask for ten gallons. It was usually two to five gallons. I heard "fifty cents' worth" many times a day. At the end of the day we usually had sold around 150 gallons. On Saturday, when everyone came to town, we would sell close to 250 gallons. We fixed a lot of flats, too, never selling a tire, just patching and booting them. The profit came from fixing flats and doing oil, grease, and wash jobs.

Dad always gave our pastor, Brother B. Dees, two cents a gallon off the price when he bought gas. Of course, he did that to other ministers as well. It doesn't seem like much, but he only made three cents per gallon profit. The two cents helped the preacher. Though Dad was not in church, he loved the church. He insisted on all of us being in church.

Mother was against me going to work at the "picture show," and the church stood against them. Also, it would keep me from going to church at night, but I rarely missed Sunday school. To Dad it was a job, and who else would hire an eleven-year-old kid?

On December 7, 1941, I was riding with my cousins, Marvin and Lavelle Cooley, who were really country boys. When we got to the only traffic light in town, it was green. They stopped and waited until it turned red and then drove on. They had a radio in the car, which was rare, and it was on. Suddenly, the program was interrupted with this message, "Pearl Harbor has been bombed by the Japanese!" What a shock! We learned later that our neighbor, J. D. Naylor, and a family friend, Dan Chelette, were on the *USS Arizona* and were both killed. It turned our world upside down! My brother Bill went to work at the shipyard in Beaumont, Texas.

Ohma was thirty years of age and possibly would not have been drafted. Bill decided to join the navy. He talked to Ohma and told him they would later draft the thirty-year-olds, so both of them decided to volunteer. Bill joined the navy and Ohma the air force. Both chose jobs in communications.

Ohma was coming home on furlough in October and then going overseas. He was radioman on a B-17 Flying Fortress. He was to be home October 4, 1943, when he was told he needed one more flight to receive his flight pay for the month, so he asked to fly the next morning—Sunday, October 3. The plane took off at his Florida base and at 6:10 AM, for some unknown reason, it crashed, killing all aboard. The air force never informed us as to the cause of the crash. His funeral was one of the largest DeRidder had ever had. African-Americans came to my father and asked if they could attend the funeral. Dad said, "By all means! You have a special invitation to attend. I will see that part of the church is saved for you." However, only a few could get into the church because the building was so small. There were over two thousand, with some reporting four thousand in attendance.

Bill was assigned to the "Sako Navy." It was called the "elite of the elite," a good name that really meant it was the most dangerous assignment to have. He was transferred behind the enemy lines in China as a guerrilla fighter. He was in the mountains above Qumoy Harbor. The average life of one of these fighters was six months. He was there eighteen months until the war was over and came home safely. He had many close calls and said "Mother's prayers" kept him alive. The Chinese government invited him back several times after the war for reunions and treated him like royalty while he was there.

My brother Orland was drafted and was later injured in the army. He died of that injury in 1950.

Medford was also drafted. He went to France after the invasion and was placed in charge of a castle in France, where he entertained congressmen and statesmen who came to France because of the war. They offered him many positions, but he refused them all.

World War II caused us to grow up fast. As soon as a boy turned eighteen, he was drafted. That caused us who were twelve to seventeen to have to shoulder the load the older ones normally carried. During those years I held two jobs, at the theater and at the service station. Rationing was in effect, and everyone had an "A" card that entitled him or her to four gallons of gas per week. The person could then apply for a "C" card that would give him or her five more gallons per week, but one had to have a good reason for a "C" card. Tires were rationed, and one had to apply to the ration board for them. It was very hard to get a permit for tires. At my age, thirteen and fourteen, many of the people who needed extra gas or tires came to me. I would fill out the proper papers, go before the ration board, and get the permits. For some reason I was never turned down, except when I went to the board for a set of tires for our car. I once had four flats in one day! I must say there were times when I became very short-tempered! I once had a flat and walked to the station, and after thirty minutes Dad asked, "Son, where is the car?"

"On a flat!" I said.

"Where?"

"On the railroad track!"

He jumped up and said, "What if a train comes?"

"I hope it does! I hope it tears that car all to pieces!"

"You go get that car right now!" He said.

We did, and the moment I let down the jack after changing the tire, I heard the train whistle. It seemed we spent a large part of our time fixing flats, and I felt like we were running on the "boots" we put in to cover the holes. We were afraid to drive the car out of town because of the tires.

One day someone stole the car, and about a week later it was found ninety miles away with a flat tire. The sheriff took me to the car, and since we couldn't start it, he pulled me back home. The car was a 1940 Ford, and we called it a "push mobile" because it often would not start. We parked it on a hill when we could in order to make it easier to push. I remember the key was broken off in the ignition and it had no windows in the doors. Sometimes it would break down between home and the station, and we would leave it there for days. One day the police called to ask Dad if a car they had found was ours. After getting it back, I decided to have it fixed up. So I put it in the shop and had glass put in the windows and shocks installed. After they finished it, I drove it around the block, and when I got back to the station, my dad had sold it. I was so disappointed and didn't even get my money back for the repairs.

He then found and bought a 1940 Chevrolet, a much nicer car than the Ford. After Dad would come to work in the mornings, I would drive the car to school and would keep it all day for my various trips. I was driving at the age of twelve. Driver's licenses were not required in Louisiana in those days. Again, we grew up fast because of the war and more was expected of us. In fact, at fifteen I was projectionist at the Realart Theater.

Our pastor, Brother Broughton Dees, had bought a new Ford just before they stopped selling them to the public in 1941, and it cost him $725. In the spring of 1944, I had just finished washing it for him and pulled it up to the gas pump when a Mr. Blankenship came into the station.

"I heard there was a truck for sale here," he said.

"Yes, sir, there was, but it sold yesterday," I answered.

Brother Dees spoke up and said, "I've got a car I'll sell you."

"How much?" he asked.

"Eight hundred dollars," Brother Dees said.

They went out to look the car over, which had a new set of tires I had gotten for Brother Dees. The man showed a great interest even though Brother Dees told him everything that was wrong with it.

"Let's go to the bank," he finally said.

A couple of hours later I saw Brother Dees walking down the street eating a bag of peanuts. I heard later that he really got the riot act read to him when he got home even though he had made a good profit on the car.

He immediately began searching for another car and found a 1936 Plymouth coupe in Shreveport. It had a lot of problems. One headlight only worked on dim, the taillight was out when the headlights were on bright, and the only brake it had was the emergency (parking) brake. One night Brother Dees was coming home when a car passed him and the driver got out and tried to flag him down. He didn't stop and this happened once more before he drove up to his house. As he was getting out of his car, the other car pulled up behind him. The driver came up to him and screamed, "Why didn't you stop when I waved at you?" He was a state policeman!

"Was that you? I don't stop for anybody who tries to stop me at night," Brother Dees said.

"You have one headlight and no taillight."

"I have two headlights and a taillight," Brother Dees said. He turned on his lights, and he had two headlights. While the policeman was walking to the back of the car, Brother Dees hit the dimmer switch and the taillight came on.

The officer apologized and said, "I would swear you only had only one headlight and no taillight!"

He then got in his car and drove off, and Brother Dees went into his house. He was at the station the next morning to get the lights repaired.

My life was in the theater. I studied it and even took the two magazines that were for theater people—Showman's Trade Review and Box Office. I knew when production started on a film and when it was completed. The manager asked my advice on how long to show movies or whether or not to show certain ones. I never missed a movie. I would always make time to see a new release. People attended the movies then because there was very little other entertainment. There would be long lines almost daily waiting for the next show to start. As a seventeen-year-old boy, I was offered my own theater, and the owners were disappointed that I turned it down. They said that if I changed my mind, they would have one ready for me. The reason I did not take the job was because I knew in my heart one day I would be in church.

I was in church every Sunday morning for Sunday school and church but would not go on Sunday or Wednesday evenings as I had to work. The real reason was that the pastor gave an altar call on Sunday evenings—never did he give one in the morning. Therefore, I felt comfortable attending church. One Sunday morning the pastor told the congregation they needed a good offering in the evening service. I thought on that and decided to give two dollars for the offering. At the same time, I decided to pay my tithes. I well remember leaving church, walking to the theater with a smile on my face, and feeling great. The next day I received a raise in pay for the amount of my tithes plus the offering—big money back then.

In the eleventh grade I decided to go out for football. However, I played very little that year because I couldn't put my heart into it. I still loved to be at the theater as much as possible, as well as the service station. When I entered the twelfth grade, I decided to really put my heart into football. The first game I was substitute left tackle. The coach pulled the player and put me in. It went that way for a game or two, and then I was on the first string. The person who had been the starting left tackle became my substitute. I will say I was pretty good at the game. I learned a lesson I have used many times in my ministry. The coach was instructing us on how to block. As tackle, I always had two men to block, but I could never do it. He became angry because I couldn't do it right, and he picked me up by my pads, set me on my feet, and said, "Let me show you how it's done!" When he showed me, I understood it. From that time on I had it. In those days at our school, we played the full game, both offense and defense. The opposing team never completed a play over me, and I could always take the players out for our team to run. I learned that being a leader is not instructing people alone; it is going before and showing them how.

Yet despite all of my success on the field, my substitute made all state instead of me and also received all the scholarships. The coach told me they had made a mistake but could not change it. He even announced in a school rally that I had starred on the football field. He and the principal told me to go on to college and go out for football, assuring me I would get a scholarship. They both said they would do everything in their power to help me. It was strange, but I can see the Lord's hand in it now.

Early in August of that year I hitchhiked to Lake Charles to enroll in McNeese College. The gentleman who gave me a ride took me right to the door of the college. I went in and was walking down the hall toward the administration office to enroll, but just as I reached the office, I heard a voice speak to me. The voice said, "Why don't you wait until the spring semester and enroll?" It sounded so real to me that I stopped, thought it over a few minutes, and then answered that voice, "OK, I will." I turned around, walked out the door, and threw up my thumb for a ride, and the first person to come by picked me up and took me to DeRidder. Shortly thereafter, I was notified that I had a job with Crosby Chemicals. A few weeks later my brother-in-law, Larry Barnhill, called me and said, "Arless, since you want a car, I will sell you my 1946 model Ford for eight hundred dollars." Cars were hard to find back then, and he was practically giving me an almost new one. It was worth twice that much. So I went to the bank at seventeen years of age and talked to the banker, who financed it for me on my own signature. When the spring semester arrived, my life had been completely turned around.

I worked two jobs at the time, seven nights a week from five to eleven at the Realart Theater and from seven to four at Crosby Chemicals. In January 1948, I went to Mr. Jenkins's office to talk to him. He had offered me my own theater a few months before. I would not accept because in my mind I knew I was going to give my life to God sometime in the future. But what an opportunity for an eighteen-year-old young man! I struggled with this for a few months. I was going to forget about God and the church and have my own life! So I said to him, "I am now ready to take that theater!"

He actually came out of his chair and said, "Wonderful! You will have it in just a few weeks!"

I left his office and said to myself, "Well, I've finally made it! I am going to do what I want to do! I do not need the church. I know it's going to make Mother sad, but she'll get over it."

Then, a week later on Tuesday, February 3, 1948, I caught up on my work at 7:45 PM. There was a revival at the church, but I was not interested in that at all. I thought of going to the other theater in town, but I had already seen the movie. I was dating a senior girl, so I called her. But she had a test the next day. So I thought, *Mother has been nagging me to go to the revival conducted by the Krauss Sisters. I think I will wait until nine when the sermon is over and they are praying at the altar. I will slip in, let Mother see me, and she won't know I wasn't there for the whole service. Then, maybe she will lay off me for a while.*

I slipped into church and sat on the back row, and to my amazement the evangelistic team was still singing. Sister Lyndal Krauss hadn't begun to preach! I wanted out, but there was no way I could walk out without my brother George who was the pastor, seeing me. He saw me come in. I sat there in utter misery while the evangelist was preaching, but I really don't think I heard a word she said. (I found out later that she was an outstanding minister. I only wanted out then!)

She concluded her message and began the altar call. That was the part I hated! She didn't even have us stand! If she had, it would have been easy just to turn and walk out. I sat there waiting for her to conclude, but it seemed as though she would never finish! That invitation went on for what seemed like a couple of hours (really it was about twenty minutes). Finally, I said to myself, *She isn't going to stop until I go to the altar!* I stood and began that long walk to the altar. On my way I stopped and asked a man, Iles, who was my barber, to join me. He refused (later he surrendered), so I continued. When I knelt at the altar, tears began to flow! My mother and brothers and sisters were thrilled beyond words. For me, the battle had just begun. The next day I worked my day job, and then I worked at the theater for a couple of hours. I went to church that night and back to the altar. It had been noised abroad. That night C. E. Cooley, my brother Charles, Orville Peters, and two or three others were there, and when I walked to the altar, they all followed me. I really thought this would blow over in a few weeks, and I would continue my life as it was. I continued going to my job at the theater and from there to the church. I saw I was getting nowhere.

Finally, the following Thursday when I finished praying, I asked my brother to let me use his phone. He wanted to know why. I said, "I am calling Mr. Jenkins and quitting my job at the theater." When I went back to the auditorium, George had told the whole church. They were rejoicing as I walked in.

When I went to the theater on Saturday for my paycheck, the theater staff met me and said, "You are quitting? You can't quit! You belong here!"

"When I walk out that door, I shall never walk in again!" I said to them.

They did not believe me. They thought I could not live without the theater. They even took bets as to how long it would be before I would return.

The following Sunday evening I was in the altar with Charles, C. E., and Orville, and C. E. received the Holy Ghost. That really irritated me! I thought, *God, I'm no bigger a sinner than C. E.! Why did you give it to him and not to me?* That made me more determined than ever!

The next night, Monday, I was the first in the altar with a number of people praying with me, including C. E. My brother Medford was praying with me when he suddenly shouted, "Here it is, Arless! Take it!" I took him at his word, and when I came to myself, I was speaking in tongues as the Spirit gave the utterance! At the same time, Charles received the Holy Ghost. When we drove home, Mother said, "Now maybe we can live with you!" Those words shocked me! I never have understood those words coming from my mother. I couldn't believe I was hard to live with, and I really believed she didn't know what she was talking about. Come to think of it, she probably wasn't talking to me but to Charles. It wasn't many more months until I received a promotion at the chemical plant that brought my salary to what it was when I worked the two jobs.

A few weeks after I received the Holy Ghost, as I was reading the Bible, I could see a "two-person God." I am by nature a little hardheaded, and I couldn't just take my mother's word or that of my brother, my pastor, either. I had to know for myself! I didn't care if there was one, three, or, as I heard a certain minister say in a debate, "When Scriptures say there is one God, it is as we would say, 'One family,' or 'One race.'" He stressed there could be a "race of gods." I wanted to know the truth. Quite often, instead of taking a lunch to work, I carried my Bible in my lunch pail. I studied it as often and as much as I could. Soon, I was promoted to a position where I could have my Bible with me at all times and had plenty of time to read and study. I wore out a Bible in one year, searching for the truth. One day, I saw it! I know now that it must be a revelation! You can have head knowledge, but until you get it in your heart, it doesn't mean a thing. Once

I received that revelation, it has been firm with me ever since. It is so beautiful to see, as Paul said in II Corinthians 5:19, "To wit [to understand], that God was in Christ [in that body], reconciling the world unto himself." I have enjoyed more than words can express preaching and teaching about the mighty God in Christ. I have found that there is a really simple explanation to any truth in the Word of God! We often make it complicated by our explanation. As Paul said in II Corinthians 11:3, ". . . simplicity that is in Christ." I know that you scholars will scoff at this, but I am just an ordinary person who wants an ordinary explanation of the Word of God. I found just two words would explain every Godhead verse in the Bible. Those two words are "Spirit" and "flesh." I know you want things more complicated, but that is the simple truth that everyone can understand. At Bethlehem the Spirit put on flesh, and that's who Jesus is, God in body.

Years later a minister friend said to me that he had a revelation on Genesis 1:26, "Let us make man in our image."

I asked him to explain it to me. He talked for at least thirty minutes, and it was profound! The only thing is I couldn't understand a word he said. I left there so disgusted with myself. I was unmerciful with me! I said, "Arless, you are undoubtedly the dumbest, most ignorant person I have ever known! A great revelation and you couldn't understand a word of it!"

I wanted to hear it again but was too ashamed to ask. A couple of weeks later, a close friend, Marvin Hicks, came to visit me. I told him about the friend having this great revelation. He wanted to hear it. I called him and asked if we could come over for him to explain it to Marvin. I listened again, we walked out, and walking to the car I asked Marvin what he thought of it.

He said, "That was tremendous! Outstanding! I never heard anything like it in my life!"

I said to him, "You hypocrite! You didn't understand a word he said!"

He answered, "I know I didn't. But wasn't that great!"

In 1945, some people left our church and started another on the other side of town. Brother L. J. Nichols was called to pastor the new church. My brother George had resigned as pastor of Faith Tabernacle in Port Arthur and was evangelizing when he was called to pastor the First Church in DeRidder. I never knew why the church split as none of my family talked about it. I really loved Brother Nichols, and his son James Dale was a good friend.

After the church was established, a young lady and her mother began attending, and both were filled with the Holy Ghost and baptized in Jesus' name. James started dating the young lady. He dated her for over a year and then broke up. For some reason James got it in his head that I was planning to date her. He was crying on my shoulder when I said to him, "Don't worry about me, James. I am not going to date her! She's not my type."

The young lady and her mother decided to leave their church and come to the First Church. By 1949 I had received the Holy Ghost and we began dating. On my next birthday she bought me a tie, and it scared me to death because she seemed to be getting serious. I broke up with her and began to date another girl in the church. I was in the air force by then and was home on a three-day pass.

On that Saturday night I was in the altar praying with someone when the Lord spoke to me and said, "She's not the one I have for you."

That shocked me, and I said, "All right, Lord; let her break up with me."

I continued praying, and the one I was praying with received the Holy Ghost. I would stay with a seeker all night if he continued, and I never left a seeker at the altar. I loved praying at the altar. Not only was I helping someone receive the Holy Ghost, but I was strengthening myself with every altar service.

I was taking the girl home when she said that she would rather wait until I was out of the service to date again. I told her that if we stopped dating now, I would never date her again.

"You will! Just wait until you are discharged and home," she answered.

At that time I was in the air force, stationed at Craig AFB in Selma, Alabama, and went home as often as possible to see my brother Orland, who was in the hospital and not expected to live. I went home on a three-day pass and decided to ask the girl who had given me the tie for a date. (At that time dating consisted of taking the girl to church and after church to get a snack and then home.) She turned me down—said she had a date! That night in church I saw her date. It was Lorene Turner (later Gustafson). That hit me hard!

She told me later that she said to Lorene she believed that I would ask for a date and she was going to turn me down. She would have the satisfaction of turning me down once even if I never called again. I went back to the base thinking, "The very idea! Home for two days and she turned me down!" I couldn't get over that and couldn't get her off my mind! I thought that if I didn't act now, someone else would win her. So I did something I didn't like to do. I wrote her a letter and told her I would be home in a couple of weeks and wanted a date with her. She accepted—so Geraldine Gill, who wasn't my type, accepted. Before I went overseas, I proposed to her. I wasn't going to take a chance of losing her.

One Sunday morning at church, my brother Bill was in church when Geri walked up to him and said, "That's a beautiful tie you're wearing."

"Why, thank you, Geri," he said.

"I gave that tie to Arless for his birthday," she answered.

Bill blushed and said, "I didn't know."

When I came home from overseas, we were married June 16, 1953. Then we went to the Louisiana camp meeting, where

I was ordained. I was talking to someone when James Nichols walked up behind me and said, "Not your type, eh!" Then he walked off without saying another word. It was a while before he would speak to me again. James was an evangelist, and every revival he conducted he preached about "the girl who broke my heart." In our evangelistic work, we would have someone walk up to Geri and say, "So you are the one who broke Brother Nichol's heart." He later married, and we became good friends again.

Nineteen forty-nine was revival year at the First Pentecostal Church. We were in revival with the Kinzie Evangelistic Team, Brother J. T. Pugh, and Brother and Sister G. A. Mangun. Each made a tremendous impact on my life, but I remember one incident that endeared me to Sister Vesta Mangun. At that time she was pregnant with Anthony, and they announced a baby shower for her. I had been only been in the church for about six months and had never heard of a baby shower. I went out and bought her a gift. The shower was at my sister Lucille's house, so I waited until almost everyone was gone and took my gift. Lucille laughed and said to me, "You crazy fool! Men don't attend baby showers! That's only for women!"

"You leave him alone!" Sister Mangun said. "Arless, I appreciate you being so thoughtful. This is so wonderful that you thought of me and my baby! I will never forget you coming with this gift."

My sister made me feel like a fool, but Sister Mangun made me feel wonderful. Of course she was always that way. If anyone could lift a person up and make him feel wonderful, it was Sister Mangun. She and her husband have been two of my favorite people from that day. Never have I met a finer, more humble man or a man I thought so much of as Gerald Mangun. Years later, Poppsy and Momsy Gibson, Vesta's parents, adopted me as their son and notified Vesta that I was her brother.

In this revival, all the evangelists made a tremendous impact on my life. Many handbills were passed out and mailed. During one of the revivals that year, someone mailed an invitation to Mrs. Fred Tenney, and she decided to attend. She talked to her son, Tom Fred, about going but he was not so keen on the idea. After a few nights he decided to come, just as we were in the altar service. The power of God was strong, but he just stood in the back watching. The power of God hit me, and I went over the pews and fell at his feet! He left!

That night he was trying to sleep but couldn't. At 4:30 AM he called his mother and said, "Call those Pentecostal people and have them pray for me; I'm dying!"

"I'm not going to do that! Go back to sleep," she answered.

He went to bed and promised the Lord, "If You will let me live until tonight, I will go to that church and go to the altar."

He was sitting on the front row with me that night, and when the altar call was given, he just fell on his knees and began praying! What a sight! He didn't receive the Holy Ghost that night. I was with him many times during the next few weeks. One night he said to Medford and me, "I've been in the altar seventeen nights, and I don't think I can receive the Holy Ghost!" That night he had finished praying, and we were all gathered around Jeanette Burkett (Glass), praying with her. Suddenly, Tom threw his hands in the air and shouted, "Glory!" He then started speaking in tongues as the Spirit gave the utterance.

We became as close as brothers after that. Every day when I got off work, either I would call him or he me and would say, "Where are we going tonight?" We went to church somewhere every night. We might drive fifty miles, but we went. When we couldn't find a church service, we would go to our church and have a prayer meeting. He is the only person I have ever heard of who wore holes in his shoes at the toes from praying.

On my twenty-first birthday, August 17, 1950, I went home from my job at the chemical plant, showered, dressed, and went to church. It was Wednesday and service began at 7:30. I arrived at about 5:30 and immediately went to the prayer room. I went to my knees and began praying, saying, "Lord, they are drafting twenty-one-year-olds and today is my birthday. What do you want me to do?" The ministry had been on my mind for about a year, and I couldn't shake it, so I was expecting a call. I wanted God to call me to work for Him or stop troubling me with it. I felt that He would call me, and then I would be exempt from military service. I was ready to go to Apostolic Bible Institute.

Much to my surprise, God spoke to me and said, "I want you to volunteer for the air force."

My answer was "No, Lord! Not the air force! My father will not allow it, and I will not go against him." (My father had lost a son and five nephews in the air force in World War II.) Then I said, "If Dad will give me permission, I will."

The Lord said to me, "I am calling you to the ministry." The call came only after I had yielded to volunteer for the air force.

At 7:30 I went to the auditorium for service, and after service, one of the most dedicated sisters in the church came up to me. She knew it was my birthday and said, "You have the call to preach, so you don't have to worry about the army."

"Oh, but I do," I said. "I am volunteering."

The next day I went to my dad and said, "Dad, I want to volunteer for the air force."

After pausing for a moment, he said, "All right, son, if you will promise me you won't get a job flying." (To this day I will not take flying lessons because of that promise.)

I went to my pastor's office and informed him that I had the call to preach. George was my pastor and my brother, and he seemed very cool to the idea. If there had been a doubt in my mind about the ministry, I would have walked out and forgotten it. He said in a very sarcastic way, "I guess now you won't have to go to the service because preachers are exempt from the military."

"I know that, but I am not claiming that exemption. I am volunteering for the air force as soon as I can make an appointment with the recruiter," I answered.

That took him by surprise, and he answered in the same way, "Well, you know you don't have to."

"But I have to," I answered. He said nothing more to me and went home that day with a long, sad look on his face. His wife knew immediately something was bothering him. She asked, "George, what is it? What's wrong?"

He said, "It's Arless! He thinks he has the call to preach!"

She said, "No, not Arless—anyone but Arless. What are you going to do?"

He answered, "I don't know!"

I don't know why she felt this way. Even though I had such a cold reception, I never wavered! There was a fellowship meeting in Ragley, Louisiana, the following Monday. I decided to attend, and I preached my first sermon there. It lasted all of five minutes. After service the pastor came to me and asked me to preach a revival for him.

To explain a fellowship meeting to those who may not be familiar with this type of service, the churches of each section came together one Monday night a month, and each pastor or preacher who attended was to preach five minutes. If one really got anointed, he or she would get to preach six minutes. The Ragley fellowship meeting was not in our section, so I knew my pastor would not attend. There was a meeting in his section that I could not attend because I went to work that night at eleven. I could make it back to work from Ragley, but I could not make it back in time from our own meeting. The next few weeks nothing more was said.

My appointment with the recruiter was September 27. On the night before, there was a fellowship meeting at Simpson, Louisiana, and even though it was my last night at home, George wanted me to go with him and Tom Tenney. We went in my car—a 1950 model.

When we drove up to the church and got out of the car, George said, "I forgot to bring my Bible!"

"Take mine," I said.

"No," he answered. "You say you have the call to preach, so you are going to preach tonight!" That was the first time he mentioned preaching to me. He went on to say, "Brother Dees, the leader, will say, 'Now we will hear from Brother Glass.' They will expect me, but you get up and go to the pulpit. You are to make no excuses about this being your first time to preach, and don't say that you are not prepared. You just open your Bible, read your Scripture, and preach."

I never said no to my pastor; I always obeyed him. Now I know what he was doing. He wanted to embarrass me so I would give up on the idea that "God had called me to preach." Brother Dees called for Brother Glass, so I walked up. He was stunned and shocked and reluctantly turned from the pulpit and walked back to his chair. I read a verse God had given me a few days earlier, and although I just had the one passage of Scripture, I opened my mouth and He began filling it. People were shouting and praising God. George and Brother Dees were crying. When I finished, the people continued to worship.

When we left the meeting, George said, "Yes, son, God has shown me that you have been called to preach! Now, I am going to see that you don't have to go to the air force."

"Oh, but I have to go, George," I said to him. "God has already spoken to me that it is His will."

TO THE AIR FORCE

So, on September 27, 1950, I boarded a Greyhound bus in DeRidder bound for the air force recruiting office in Alexandria, Louisiana. One of my lifelong friends, Maxwell Chelette, went with me. Much to our surprise, he was rejected and I was accepted. Later, he was drafted into the army. I soon boarded a train for San Antonio, Texas, where we were housed in tents because there were no barracks available. Before boarding the train, I called home and told my mother I was accepted. She informed me that Molly, Bill's wife, had just given birth to a baby boy. It was mighty hard to say good-bye to Mother.

I was a "cornbread and buttermilk" eater. I didn't eat chicken, green beans, squash, butter, smothered steak, or a lot of other things. Now I was on a train and I was hungry! The air force had given us a meal ticket for the train. When it was announced that dinner was being served, I went to the dining car and picked up a menu. The waiter informed me that the only food they were serving was cream of chicken on toast. I shuddered! Then I thought, *Old boy, this isn't mother's table. They don't care whether you eat or not, so you may as well make up your mind that you are going to eat it!* I told him to bring it on! I took one look at it and wanted to shove it back, but I knew I couldn't. So reluctantly I started eating. I discovered that it was good! I then made up my mind that I would eat anything set before me. For several days the food that was served would have turned my stomach at home, but this was the air force. I had to eat, so eat I did.

The first few days at San Antonio, we went through the processing procedure, which consisted of a lot of standing in line and being harassed and yelled at. I well remember the third night. We had gotten to bed around eleven, and at one o'clock they sounded the bugle. We hit the floor, made our bunks, and fell out in formation. They then proceeded to march us to the supply warehouse, where we were each issued a pair of tennis shoes, and then they marched us back to our tents. We never wore those tennis shoes after that! As a matter of fact, I still have them, and they are nothing like those of today. After a week in San Antonio, we loaded a bus for Shepherd AFB in Wichita Falls, where we began our basic training.

I still remember my flight number. It was 5522, and our drill instructor's name was Corporal Britt. In the process of our training, the air force gave us a series of aptitude tests to determine what we were best qualified to do. Of the nine tests, I scored very high on seven and high on the other two, so I was competent to train in any field they needed. I was given permission to talk to the wing chaplain and requested to work in the chaplaincy. When I got my orders, there was a note across my records that said "Chaplaincy," and that started a very interesting chapter of my life.

Most of us felt that they were not giving us enough to eat in the mess hall. We all left hungry, and there was much complaining among us. We talked to our drill instructor about it but nothing happened, and we surmised that he was afraid to go higher up the chain of command. Some of us had tried to go back for more but were always refused.

Finally, one day I finished my tray, turned it in, and decided to get another tray and go back through the chow line. One of my buddies saw me and asked me if I had already eaten. When I said I had, he said to me, "You're going to get in trouble."

"Yes, but I'm still hungry, and I'm going back through," I answered.

Sure enough, the mess officer heard me and came to me and asked, "Haven't you eaten?"

"Yes, sir, but I'm still hungry."

"Come with me," he said. He took me to the kitchen and put me to washing trays.

Another buddy saw me and asked, "What are you doing back there?"

"Can you get Corporal Britt?" I asked him.

Corporal Britt came and told me to get outside and join my flight. I soon found myself in the squadron commander's office.

"What is the problem?" the commander asked.

"Sir, when I volunteered for the air force, they promised that I would be fed and clothed. The portions of food they give me in the chow hall are not enough, and I'm always hungry when I leave there. They only gave me a small portion, and I went back for more and was refused. I turned the tray in and got a clean one, and when the mess officer saw me, he took me to the kitchen and put me to washing trays. None of us is satisfied with the amount of food they serve us."

"Is that it?" he asked.

"Yes, sir."

He then dismissed me. The next day when we went to chow, the same officer met us at the door and said, "If you do not get enough to eat, bring your tray back for more."

From that time we always had plenty to eat. I learned that someone had to stand up for our rights, and even though it was a rough experience, it was worth it.

After completing basic training, I was assigned to Craig AFB in Alabama, where I was classified as a "Welfare Specialist," the air force title for a chaplain's assistant. I testified to everyone who would listen, and one I witnessed to was Sergeant Guy Bowie, a Methodist minister. We worked in the same office and went to chow together every day. We had Sunday morning services at the base chapel, and since there was no United Pentecostal church in Selma, I began attending church in Montgomery, Alabama, with Brother Joe Lane on Sunday nights. I would usually take a carload with me. One evening I asked Guy to go with me. Despite our friendship, Guy did not agree with me on the message of salvation at all, and we had many interesting discussions.

One morning as we went to eat, he said to me, "God showed me last night how beautiful the Trinity is. It was so clear how there are three persons in the Godhead."

"Explain it to me," I said.

He started his explanation and then said, "I don't remember how it was, but it was so beautiful. I don't remember a word of it."

After a few weeks we drove to DeRidder, Louisiana, where my brother George baptized Guy in Jesus' name and he was filled with the Holy Ghost.

I sometimes preached in the First Methodist Church in downtown Selma, Alabama, and also was invited to preach in the Fire Baptized Pentecostal Church. During this time the Alabama District had a conference at Florence, Alabama, and I was privileged to go. Brother Benson was the pastor of that church. I remember that Brother Howard Goss was there as a headquarters representative. I had met him one time in DeRidder, and to hear him pray would make the hair stand up on your head. What a Christian and what a prayer warrior! When he prayed, we knew that every word went directly to the throne of God. Later, I commented to my mother about the way he could pray and she said that was the way all those pioneers prayed. During the time I spent there, I really fell in love with the Alabama District and with Brother Joe Lane. He was one of a kind! After being discharged from the air force, I went back to Montgomery and preached a revival. That is where I met one of the best friends I have ever had, James Lumpkin. He and his wife, Jean, became an important part of our lives from that time.

At the base chapel, I was assigned a Sunday school class of teenagers. They had no lesson material, so I began using my own United Pentecostal literature. I showed it to the other teachers, and they all wanted it, too. One of the teachers took the literature to the wing chaplain and said, "This is the best literature I have ever seen. I think we should use it throughout our Sunday school program." I'm not sure he appreciated that as they were using the Lutheran literature. On Easter Sunday I taught a lesson on the Cross and the Resurrection. Some of the young people were moved to tears and were thrilled with the lesson. They went home and told their parents, and some of the parents resented this. They called the wing chaplain and said they did not appreciate teachings in the chapel that would cause their children to cry. I heard nothing of this until an order came for an overseas assignment for a chaplain's assistant. The wing chaplain immediately submitted my name. He was told that I was overqualified for the assignment, but he insisted. My chaplain called me aside one day and told me, "You will make a great preacher if you will change your message. You will never get anywhere preaching the message you now preach." Later when I was sitting in my tent in Okinawa, in the pouring rain with the tent leaking, discouraged and about to cry, suddenly his words came back to me. I thought, *Never get anywhere? I think I did pretty well. I made it ten thousand miles from home!* I brightened up and was all right from that day on.

God does work in mysterious ways. I left basic training at Sheppard AFB to be stationed at Craig AFB and was granted a "delay in route" to visit my brother Orland who was dying in the hospital. He was injured in WWII, and we thought he was healed until the injury resurfaced in June 1950. I also wanted to pick up my car so I would have transportation. Somehow my records got lost and did not make it to Craig. After a month of searching, they finally created new records. The air force has "specialty codes" to designate skill levels—thirty for trainees, fifty for completely skilled, and seventy for supervisory personnel. When they filled out the new file on me, they put me in the fifty category. This helped me in my future assignments and in obtaining rank.

One weekend, I took a three-day pass and drove to Tupelo, Mississippi, to visit C. E. Cooley, who was a student at the Bible college there. We grew up together, and he is like a brother to me. I tease him a lot when I get the chance about how I once visited him in jail. His face always turns red, and the audience is shocked. I then say, "His father was the jailer, and they lived in the same building as the jail." I just had to do the same thing when I was at the Bible college when he introduced me to Brother Soper, president of the college. I was asked to preach at the chapel service, and after the service, a number of students gathered around me and began asking questions. Since the semester was nearly over, many of them were interested in what I knew about their being drafted. I said, "You men are worried about the draft? I'm not." I was in uniform. They didn't think that was very funny.

One of the young men in the reserves said, "If I have to go back to the army, I may as well give up in the beginning because I know I won't be able to make it as a Christian." That summer he was in an automobile accident and was killed. The next day he received a summons to report for duty.

It has been proven many times that you can live for God in the military. It is a mind-set. Just make up your mind, and you can live for God anywhere in the world. You can do a great work for God in the military. I've heard it said that when a person prays at his or her bedside, they will kick you and make fun of you. I found none of that to be true. I prayed every morning and night, kneeling at my bunk. I read my Bible openly where all could see. No one made fun of me, but many did come to talk to me. One young man asked if he could partner with me because he didn't want to forsake his Christian upbringing. Many others asked me for advice. One evening, one of the men came from the upper bay of the barracks and asked if I would come up and read the Bible to them. I went up, and the entire bay was around me listening to me read. Then we talked about the Lord for hours. I had the respect of my entire flight, including our flight leader.

When I was informed that I had orders to go overseas, I didn't want to go. I went to chow from work, back to the office, and then to the Sunday school room to pray. I planned to pray all night and just knew that God would get me out of the assignment. My first words were, "O Lord, I don't want to go overseas."

Then the Lord answered me in what I thought was an audible voice, "But, son, I want you to go."

"That's good enough for me, Lord," I said. I got off my knees and went to my office and began studying the Bible. My prayer meeting that was to last all night did not last five minutes! The Lord gave me a sermon, and I began writing it. When I finished, I asked, "Why, Lord?" He didn't answer.

When I reported for duty the next morning, I received a call from the orderly room, asking me to come there. The first sergeant said, "Glass, the CO (commanding officer) wants to talk to you. He wants to cancel the orders for you to go overseas at this time. He has searched for something against this chaplain and feels he has it with his railroading you to this overseas assignment." (This chaplain was the most corrupt chaplain I ever met. He was an embarrassment to all who knew him and worked with him.)

"No, Sergeant, I have to go sometime, and it may as well be now," I answered.

"But the Far East? That's the worst assignment we have. The next request could be for Germany. Germany is a cream puff." I stood firm.

I had heard from God and knew this was His will.

Two days later a Methodist church called and wanted a preacher Sunday morning, and for some unknown reason they asked for me. I had the sermon, and God anointed me wonderfully. My text was from Hebrews 2:1, "Drifting from the truth." I did not offend anyone yet preached the truth with the congregation asking me to come back again. My pastor, my brother George, taught me that I am always safe if I stay with the Bible. People will always listen. I have proven that to be true so many times. I went home for a ten-day leave preparatory to leaving for my new assignment to the Far East.

TO OKINAWA

On the last Sunday morning of June 1951, I was driving the fifty miles to the airport in Lake Charles, Louisiana, for my flight to San Francisco, California. I was to report to Camp Stoneman to be processed for my overseas assignment. This was my first time to fly, and I was looking forward to it. Normally, I would have traveled by train but had wanted to stay home as long as possible. So I elected to fly, and it was a memorable flight. The man who drove me to the airport dropped me off and went immediately back to DeRidder in order to be in Sunday school and church.

I went to the check-in counter, and the gentleman weighed my luggage. He whistled and said, "Forty-five pounds overweight. That will be an extra forty-five dollars."

"I don't have forty-five dollars," I told him. But that made no difference. I walked away from the counter, then walked back and said, "I have to have all my luggage because I am going overseas."

"Let me see your orders," he asked, "These orders will allow you an extra twenty-five pounds, so you only have to pay for an extra twenty pounds."

I had a portable phonograph that I had bought for nineteen dollars in Alabama, and it weighed exactly twenty pounds. I didn't even have to think about it. I paid the twenty dollars to take it and all my 45 RPM records of the Blackwood Brothers.

We flew to Dallas and then boarded a plane to San Francisco. We hit bad weather twenty minutes out of Dallas and were forced to return. After a nine-hour delay, we left again. The plane developed engine trouble, and we had a forced landing at El Paso. I was a day late getting to Camp Stoneman and was listed as AWOL. The airlines gave me a letter explaining the delay, which got me off the AWOL list. The phonograph was nothing but trouble all the way. I had to carry it in my hand, along with my duffel bag and B4 bag, and it was almost impossible to carry it all. Another airman who was on the same flight offered to help, and he was a godsend.

In San Francisco I was put into a holding flight awaiting transportation. I saw with some trepidation that my orders read, "Destination: EVIL." On my first day in the holding flight barracks, I was sitting on my bunk and unpacked my phonograph and began playing records. I thought I was alone in the barracks when a tall airman walked up to me and said, "I like that music; mind if I listen?"

He was Clifford (Gus) Gustafson, and we soon got into a conversation about the Lord. He finally said, "Look, I'm Presbyterian, and I have all the religion I need. I go to church maybe once every three or four months, and that's all I need." He then turned and walked away. I thought that would be the last time I would see him.

We were in formation each morning and were assigned duty. I was given KP duty every other day, and who was next to me—Gus. So we worked and I talked. At break I would pull out my New Testament and read. He said, "What are you going to do when you finish reading it? I know you're going to read it again." Groups would gather around me in the barracks, and I would talk. They were full of questions. The lights would be turned out at eleven, but we continued to talk, sometimes going until two in the morning. Gus would never join the discussions. I found men very hungry for the Lord. There were times when everyone in the bay, fifty-five men, gathered around me, and I would testify to them about the love of God. Gus shipped out two weeks before me, and he was privileged to fly while I had to go by ship.

I had many experiences while at Camp Stoneman, testifying to everyone who was interested. When our travel orders came, they issued us a weapon, helmet, and field pack with the rumor we were going to Korea and to the front lines. The night before shipping out, I was on my bunk when about five bunks from me an airman started reading the Bible aloud. He would read a couple of words and insert a curse word. The entire upper bay was full of men, about fifty including two rooms where the NCOs stayed. I listened as he read and cursed. After a few minutes I got up, walked over to him, and said, "I appreciate you reading the Bible, but I don't like the way you are reading it. We are leaving in the morning, and orders read, 'Destination EVIL.' The very reason we are going is because of a lack of respect for that Book."

I preached him a very short sermon and walked back to my bunk. That was one of the longest walks I ever made. I walked slowly but really wanted to run, halfway expecting him and others to jump me and beat me up. The man I rebuked got up, walked outside the barracks, and in about five minutes came back in, walked up to me, and said, "We are going over and have no idea where, and it's going to be an experience." Then he asked me a Bible question. I answered it, and others began to gather around me. Soon everyone in the upper bay was around me, including the NCOs, all asking questions about the Bible. Others came from downstairs, and for two hours they asked questions and God gave me the answers. The Lord was letting me know that if I would take my stand, He would work miracles among the men.

We boarded the *USS Patrick* and for fourteen days traveled to Okinawa. The time was, for me, enjoyable. I assisted the naval chaplain in services and testified to everyone who would listen, every day and most of every night. After the lights were out, I would go up on deck with a group and talk for hours about the Lord Jesus Christ. I loved it!

One I had talked to while in the holding flight was Jeep Dabbs. He worked in the motor pool, thus his nickname "Jeep." We were eating chow, and in front of us were two airmen arguing. They started to fight when Jeep said to me, "Give me your Bible." He took the Bible, placed it between the two, and said, "Now, fight!" When they saw the Bible, they shook hands, sat down, and the fight was over. Jeep had never been to church in his life but was hungry to hear the Word. When we boarded ship, I spent as much time as I could witnessing to him.

One night I was on deck, and Jeep came to me and said, "There's a man in my bay called Morgan; he says he is Assembly of God Pentecostal. What difference is there between you?"

"Well, Jeep, he believes there are three persons in the Godhead, and I believe there's only one; that is, Jesus."

I then prepared for a long discourse on the Oneness when he said to me, "Let's get this straight. He believes there are three persons in the Godhead, and you believe there is only one?"

"Yes."

"He's crazy!"

I didn't know what to make of that answer and said, "What do you mean?"

"He believes there are three up there? He's crazy!" Then he said, "Listen, things are running too smooth for there to be three up there!" I thought that was a pretty good observation.

When our ship docked at Okinawa, I was met by a special vehicle and taken to Headquarters, 20th Air Force. On the way I saw a sign, "Youth for Christ meets here." I set my cap to preach at one of those services as soon as possible. I was taken to the office of the chief of chaplains, and when I went in he stood up, looked me over, then said, "Where am I going to put you?" Needless to say, that was somewhat discouraging. Then he said, "Chaplain Hurley, who is Catholic, has a man on TDY (temporary duty) from the army. We will send him back to the army and have you as his assistant." Chaplain Hurley was called, and he came immediately for me. He was with the 307th Bomb Wing, and I was assigned to the 6332nd Wing, which meant that I was permanent party with a two-year assignment. The 307th was on temporary duty wing. They lived in tents and rotated every six months. Have you ever lived in a tent? I mean for six months? I later lived in a tent during the rainy season, which lasted six months, and my tent leaked. I got some lumber and built a shed over my bunk, putting another tarp over the shed, and because of that I could at least keep my bed dry.

My tent inside a tent

Three soldiers who received the Holy Ghost and I baptized

Chaplain Hurley asked me what my denomination was. I told him, "United Pentecostal." His jaw dropped, and he then said he would honor my convictions and not ask me to do anything against them. He did not say another word, and I wondered why. I went through records of the day-to-day journal and found that the Pentecostals (Assemblies of God) had given him a lot of trouble. I was told that everyone called him "Little Caesar" because he was so difficult to work with. No assistant had ever pleased him. I determined to do my job as he outlined it as long as it did not interfere with my own convictions. One day, he gave me some letters to type. I noticed he had misspelled a number of words but typed them exactly as he had spelled them. I then placed his copy with mine and put them on his desk. He soon called out to me, "You've made some mistakes." Then he looked at his copy and saw that he had made them. He corrected his mistakes and said with a smile, "You'll have to type this over." It was double work, but since I had to work my quota of hours anyway, I didn't mind.

One day he called me to his office and said, "Corporal Glass, I'm putting you in for another stripe. Every assistant I have had always corrected my letters. Sometimes I wrote in Latin, and they corrected that, too. I didn't like that at all. You type it exactly as I write it, and I like that. You don't belong in my office; you belong in headquarters. I'm going to write a letter for you to give them, and you will be transferred to Tokyo." I never used the letter because the tour of duty in Tokyo was three years and Okinawa was two. I wasn't about to ask for another year of duty there. He got me the stripe, though—Buck Sergeant. Considering I had been in the air force for only eleven months, this was almost unheard of. It was supposed to take at least thirty-five months. I saw the hand of God taking care of me.

My main job was writing letters to the next of kin of men killed in action. There were four letters for each man, two letters each sent to the two next of kin listed on his records. One was called Letter on Circumstance. The commanding officer would send me the circumstances that caused the death and expressing sympathy for the loss, and I would then write a letter for him to sign. Next I would write a letter of condolence for the chaplain to sign. The B-29 bombers had a crew of eleven and sometimes twelve, and when one was shot down, that meant a lot of letters. There were seven carbon copies, and they had to be perfect with no erasures or strike-outs. The typewriters were manual, which didn't help. To make it more nerve-racking, I only had three days to complete them. They could not in any way sound like a form letter and had to be worded differently because the crews were all from McDill AFB in Florida, and sometimes the families would compare letters. The letters had to be personal, and copies went all the way to the Pentagon. Oh, the paper I used before I was able to type a perfect letter!

Me standing in front of Tent City

October 22, 1951, was one of the most tragic days for us who were on Okinawa during the entire Korean War. The 19th Bombardment Group and the 307th Bombardment Wing were both on temporary duty from the States, there for the purpose of bombing North Korea. Both of these groups were made up of B-29 Super Fortresses, and they flew seven days a week. Each B-29 carried a payload of thirty-nine, five-hundred-pound bombs. There was so much weight that they had to fly at tree-top level for several miles until they could gain altitude. There was also a group of B-50s assigned to the base, and these were more powerful than the B-29s. These were there in case we would be forced to drop atomic bombs, which were in storage on the base. Altogether, our bombers dropped over three million tons of bombs in North Korea.

On at least one occasion while I was there, it seemed we would be forced to use a nuclear weapon. We were all restricted to base, and events were being watched closely. China's army marched to the Manchurian border, and thousands of troops crossed into North Korea. They entered the war but were defeated in the battles at first. Untold thousands were killed. Reports said that the first wave would throw themselves onto the barbed-wire barricades and would all be killed by machine gun and rifle fire. The second wave walked over the dead bodies to get over the barbed wire and kept coming. Our soldiers killed so many that the Chinese literally would have to walk over their dead comrades, but they just kept coming. Our soldiers' machine guns were fired so rapidly and for so long that the barrels actually began to melt. We were afraid that more of the Chinese army would cross the border and enter the war, so the group was notified to prepare to use nuclear bombs to stop them. The Chinese withdrew.

Getting back to October 22, 1951, we sent nine B-29s from the 307th Bomb Wing to the Yalu River to bomb a hydroelectric plant. They were under orders not, for any reason, to cross the Yalu River. Across the river was Manchuria, and we were not at war with them even though the North Korean air base was located across the river. Our airmen could see the planes flying from the bases, coming to attack them. Our bomber crews were ordered to "lay your eggs and come home." This area was called "Mig Alley" (Migs being Russian fighter planes) even though they would hardly ever attack our bombers. Once in a while a plane would attack, but it was extremely rare because our bombers were escorted by F-86s. Usually we lost a plane about every six weeks, and this was mainly due to mechanical failure or running out of fuel. On this particular day, however, the escort fighters were F-80s, which were mainly used as training planes at this time. They said, "Let's rest the 86s. We never need them." When the bombers neared the target, the pilots looked up and saw what they estimated to be at least 150 Mig-15s diving on the formation. The gunners did the best they could, but the F-80s fought a losing battle because they were so badly outnumbered. They just about destroyed all our planes! Of the nine planes that we sent over the target, eight were badly damaged. Only one, shot to pieces, made it back to Okinawa with dead and wounded aboard. The skill of the pilot brought it home, and I watched it circle a couple of times before he decided to land. After it landed, it was in such bad condition that it never flew again.

Of the eight planes lost, two crashed in the China Sea and their crews were rescued; two more landed in South Korea although all of them were shot to pieces. I never knew how many fighter pilots were lost, but I got a list of the forty-eight men from our base who were lost on this raid. A nineteen-year-old airman came to me with tears in his eyes and said, "Arless, you almost had to write my folks this time!"

It seemed a "funeral pall" hung over the base for weeks because of the loss of so many friends. They had to bring in new planes and crews from the States to replace those lost. We painted the new planes black underneath and began flying nothing but night missions from that day forward. In the investigation of why we lost so many planes, they decided that the main reason was that they were flying so far apart that the enemy could get in between them. After that, the orders were to fly in "close formation"—to get as close to each other as possible to prevent the enemy from getting among us. This is so much like the words of Jesus, "Where two or three are gathered together in my name, there am I in the midst of them" (Matthew 18:20).

We were sent a stateside newspaper with the headlines: "One hundred fifty Migs attack Super Fortresses in greatest air battle in air history." The story stated that we lost one plane, and one crashed in the China Sea and the crew was rescued. Later someone from Okinawa wrote *Time* magazine with the true story, but they would only print the letter in the Letters to the Editor section. Yet I had to type ninety-six letters of condolences to the families of the airmen killed.

A B-29 Superfortress ready for mission

A B-29 carried thirty-nine of those five hundred pound bombs

When the list of the forty-eight names was brought to me, I told them it was impossible for me to have the 192 letters ready in three days. The commanding officer had the best typist from each orderly room come, bring his typewriter, and type them with me. We started at eight in the morning, and when five o'clock came, they had only typed one good letter. The pile of discarded paper reached nearly to the ceiling. I wound up typing every one over, but the officer did extend the deadline for two days.

Now, let me tell a little about my spiritual activities while on Okinawa. The first Saturday I was there I decided to go to the Youth for Christ service. As I was waiting for the bus, several others came up, going to the same place. I saw a master sergeant (Wheeler), walked over to him, and struck up a conversation. He was the Pentecostal who had given the chaplain so much trouble. When I told him I was United Pentecostal, he backed away from me and didn't say a word. We caught the bus and went to the service.

They had a testimony service that evening, which they had never had before and never had one after. I testified, and God anointed me. The man in charge of the service, Missionary Bell, a Methodist missionary, came to me after the service and said, "You are a preacher, aren't you? I want you to preach the first Saturday in September."

Sergeant Wheeler went back to his tent, and the next night as he was conducting his Bible class, he told his group, "There's a devil on this island, and his name is Glass. He doesn't believe in the Trinity. He believes that damnable doctrine of Oneness, that Jesus is the only God. Stay away from him." His class consisted of four Okinawan ladies who worked on the base and about that many airmen. One of the airmen, Bill Gray, left that meeting, and since he was off the next day, he decided to come to my office to convert me. He was a crew member of a B-29, bombing Korea almost every day. He intended to spend the entire day with me, and since my duties on that day allowed me to talk to him and still do my job, it worked out well. He arrived at 8:00 AM, and at 4:00 PM we walked to the China Sea, where I baptized him. He was, I believe, the first person ever baptized in Jesus' name on the island of Okinawa. The date was around August 15, 1951. When he heard about it, Sergeant Wheeler told his group, "Bill is lost for sure now."

Bill and I happened to go to the PX together the next week, and Sergeant Wheeler saw us. He walked over and began to run me down. For what seemed like an hour, he called me every bad name he could think of, even using slang and mild curse words. He cursed my doctrine and said it was of the devil, straight from the pit of Hell. I just stood there listening. Finally he ran out of things to say, and I said with a smile, "I'll see you later, Sergeant Wheeler."

We started to walk away when Sergeant Wheeler called, "Bill."

"Yes, Sergeant?" Bill answered.

"Did you see that? When Chandler (an Assembly of God preacher) and I had a falling out, he went away mad and hasn't spoken to me since. But Glass leaves with a smile. Stick with him; he's got something."

Bill Gray, the first man baptized in Jesus' name on Okinawa

We had a five-day typhoon in mid-August. No work could be done, so I had plenty of time to study and pray. I asked the Lord to "let me be the best preacher these people have ever heard." I knew they had never heard a Jesus'-Name-Holy-Ghost preacher before. Billy Graham had preached there, as well as E. Stanley Jones and several other popular preachers of that time. God did not let me down! The words flowed for forty minutes, and the audience was sitting on the edge of their seats. After the service they thronged me! One of the soldiers, Sergeant Kenneth Fields, came with a big smile and said, "I haven't heard preaching like that since I left home." I said, "You are Pentecostal." He answered that he attended a Pentecostal church in the States.

The chaplain who was giving Bible studies daily asked me to fill in for him on the following Tuesday, and I asked Kenneth to be sure to come. Bill Gray had not attended the previous meeting because he was on CQ (Charge of Quarters) duty that night. Sergeant Wheeler went to him and began condemning me for not preaching on the Holy Ghost. My message was: "Remove not the ancient landmark, which thy fathers have set" (Proverbs 22:28)—

how man is trying to remove the virgin birth, the miracles, the value of His blood, His resurrection, and so on. (I have tried to preach that message again, but I can never get it the way God gave it to me that night!)

"He had his chance to tell all of them that they needed the baptism of the Holy Ghost, but he didn't!" Sergeant Wheeler argued. He did not know I had walked in and heard him.

"Sergeant Wheeler," I spoke up, "you want to hear a message on the Holy Ghost? The chaplain asked me to take his service Tuesday evening. You be there, and I will preach you a message on the Holy Ghost."

Tuesday evening I dismissed the chaplain's service early and started my own Bible study. Sergeant Wheeler brought his entire group, Kenneth Fields brought some men with him, and a few others who were in the Youth for Christ service attended—twenty-three people in all.

Before the service began, I told Sergeant Wheeler that the chaplain had called and refused to baptize the Okinawans who attended his service. He said an Okinawan pastor needed to baptize them. He looked at me strangely and turned away. We started the service, and I taught four and one-half hours on the Tabernacle plan. Of the twenty-three there, I baptized seventeen of them.

The next night when Sergeant Wheeler had his Bible study, the four Okinawans stood and said to him, "We no listen to you any longer. Get Corporal Glass; we listen to him." He came to me and asked if I would baptize these four. Naturally, I said I would be happy to. We walked to the China Sea, and the first one in the water was Sergeant Wheeler, followed by the Okinawans. His other members were also baptized, along with Kenneth Fields and his friends. What a day!

Sergeant Wheeler came to me and said, "I have always heard that you Oneness people were devils, but I have watched you and knew you had something I did not have. I told the Lord,

'I have asked the chaplain to baptize these girls. I want him to refuse. After they hear Corporal Glass, I want them to refuse to listen to me any longer.'"

When Sergeant Wheeler was rotated back to the States, he testified to the group and said, "I thought Sergeant Glass was all wrong in the way he approached the message of salvation, and I condemned him. But I now can say he was right in his approach. He won me, you, and many others. My way was wrong, and I thank God for the way He led Sergeant Glass in his ministry."

A couple of those who walked out of that earlier Bible study began spreading rumors that I preached there was no Christ (that is, after I preached for forty minutes about Jesus at the Youth for Christ service). The four and one-half hours I taught was proving Jesus was God, yet the rumors continued. I was the topic of conversation over the Christian community, and they were fighting me as hard as they could.

A group was at the Naha AFB chapel in a Bible study when Gus walked in and asked, "Who did you say he is?"

"Glass," they said. "Stay away from him. He preaches that there is no Christ!"

"Not the Glass I know! That's all he can talk about. Where is he?"

They told him, and the next day he called me. He said, "Hello, Art. This is Gus. Remember me?"

I didn't, but I didn't want him to know it. I said, "Hello Gus! How are you doing?"

"I am off tomorrow," he then said. "Can I come over?"

The next morning I was driving to the motor pool, and I saw him walking from the bus stop. I recognized him immediately and pulled over, and he got into the jeep. The first thing he said was, "Say, about that speaking in tongues, I don't believe it!"

We talked for a long time, and at the end of the day we walked to the China Sea so I could baptize him! I was stationed at Kadena AFB, and he was about thirty miles from me at Naha

AFB. We were together every Saturday and at our Monday night service. He brought some airmen to our Monday night service who received the Holy Ghost. He became discouraged because he had not received the Holy Ghost and said, "I can't understand it! I bring them with me, and they receive the Holy Ghost but I can't!" A couple of services later he received the Holy Ghost.

When we had an approaching typhoon, I would be issued a number of cases of C-rations. Once I opened a case, I could not return it. A case had forty-eight boxes. I kept these in my room, and after Bible classes we would all go to my room, which was in back of the chapel, and eat. We could have gone to the mess hall, but it wouldn't have been nearly as much fun as being in my room. I always had plenty to eat, thanks to the C-rations. "C" means cook rations. We would heat them and many times eat them from the cans. We thought they were delicious. Geri would send me a box about once a month that included cake, candy, cookies, a box of Hi-Ho crackers, and a pecan pie. I looked forward to the box coming. The others looked forward to it too, so I had to share. The box would get there about the time the men came over for Bible class. Many times they would bring someone over for me to talk to, and while I talked, they would help themselves to my goodies. When I finished my lesson, they had finished the food. They would say, "We're sorry, but we ate every bit of your box from Geri!" Then they would have a big laugh. I can still see John Concesico wadding up the bag, throwing it in the garbage, and saying, "That's finished." Then he would smile and say, "I'm so sorry we ate all your food." Those were wonderful times, and all of our talk was about the Lord.

Clifford Gustafson was a remarkable person! I loved him as my own brother, and he adopted me as the brother he never had. He and I volunteered for the air force the same day. The train they put him on came through Alexandria, and I boarded it. We went to Sheppard AFB together, where he was in flight 5521 and I was in flight 5522. We finished basic training together. He went to Keesler AFB, Mississippi, and I went to Craig AFB, Alabama. We got orders to go overseas on the same day and arrived at Camp Stoneman the same day, but we had never met until the day I was playing my phonograph with the Blackwood Brothers singing. God moves in mysterious ways His wonders to perform! I am still amazed! Gus had a brilliant mind. His father was the number-three man in Standard Oil of New Jersey, and his mother was a former model in New York City. His sister was married to a wonderful Jewish man.

On Okinawa Gus was assigned to Aircraft Control, directing air traffic. While in the tower they had shortwave radios and would sometimes listen to various stations. One day his relief entered the tower, and the propaganda station was on. He said to Gus, "How can you listen to that stuff without it bothering you?"

Gus said, "It doesn't bother me at all, you dirty capitalist swine." They all had a good laugh about that.

Gus and I were together as much as possible, and that was true of all of us. The beautiful thing is that we were always talking about the Lord. As far as we were concerned, that was heavenly. Once Gus received the Holy Ghost, it was as if he had been Pentecostal all his life. I was thrilled at the way he grasped the message and proclaimed it! At our Monday night services, he brought his guitar, and that was our music. We were thankful for that. I was the song leader and thought I did a pretty good job. At any rate, nobody complained. When it came time for a special song, I would get Gus to sing, and he would usually ask me to join him. So we sang duets, and the group asked for more. I'm sure it was because of Gus's voice and not mine! I didn't complain and loved to hear Gus sing. I tried to get him to sing "Wayfaring Pilgrim" at every service. He let me know that he knew more songs than that but would always do it for me. Years later when we came home and he preached revivals for me, I would request that song as often as I could.

When we started working with Brother Tokeshi, we saw he needed transportation. He walked from village to village preaching. When he could, he caught a bus, but that did not happen often. Gus found a used Cushman scooter for sale, which was a rarity as transportation was scarce on the island. There was no way we could buy a new one that would have to be shipped from the States or Japan. Besides that, we could not afford that. The owner wanted $188 for the used scooter. It looked pretty beat up, but Gus felt that he could work it over so it would be usable. I wrote home to my brother and pastor, George, and told him about it. I did not write expecting anything; it was just that I always tried to keep him informed about what we were doing. He mentioned it to the Foreign Missions Board, and Brother Abbott from Canada sent us a check. That was a godsend. We purchased the scooter, and Gus took it to the base to work it over. He would ride it to my base on the weekends, but it needed a kickstand. When he stopped, he would have to prop it against something. Such parts could not be found.

One Monday evening he met me at my office, and we got into the jeep to go to the old, deserted chapel on the hill for service. As we were driving along, I hit a piece of metal in the road. I stopped, and Gus asked me why I had stopped. I said, "That is the kickstand we need." He laughed and thought I was kidding, and the others joined in. Gus got out and went back to where we hit it, and sure enough, it was a kickstand for a Cushman scooter! Unbelievable! None of us could believe it, but it was. God was taking care of us. Gus put it on, and the scooter was ready for Brother Tokeshi. We delivered it to him, and the tears flowed. Gus taught him to ride it, and when we left a year later he was still going strong on the scooter.

Me on our motor scooter

Clifford Gustafson and John Concesico

While we were in Okinawa, Gus brought an airman, Bobby Massey from Georgia, with him to our church service. He was a farm boy, and the other airmen nicknamed him "Zeke." Gus and Zeke were in the habit of going to a stateside restaurant every Saturday for a root beer float. Zeke received the Holy Ghost on a Monday, and the following Saturday they went to this restaurant and sat at the counter.

"Gus, do you think we ought to?" Zeke asked.

"Ought to what?"

"Order a root beer float! After all, it's got 'beer' in it!"

"Why, Zeke, I imagine many times back home you had 'pot liquor,' didn't you?"

"That's right," Zeke answered and then said to the waitress, "Give us two root beer floats."

Gus was a tremendous soulwinner, and almost every week he would bring someone new to the service or to my room behind the chapel for me to talk to. He would eat my food while I talked to the person, and he especially liked Geri's pecan pie (he pronounced it Pea-can). We would use any form of transportation we could secure for attending our Bible classes or church services. One night Gus and the group from Naha AFB came in a big truck, and that was the night Zeke received the Holy Ghost. When it came time to leave the service, Zeke was still on the floor, speaking in tongues, so Gus and some of the others picked him up, loaded him in the back of the truck, and drove to their base. I never thought to ask how they got in the gate! Another night they went to the Naha beach to pray and crawled up on a huge rock. They got carried away in their praying, and the tide came in, surrounding the rock. They had to swim to shore. Some other airmen questioned why they were swimming with their clothes on. I must admit while I am writing this, I get so lonesome for what used to be!

After Gus received the Holy Ghost, I said, "Gus there's a girl at home I would like for you to write."

"Give me her name and address, and I'll write," he said.

I gave him Lorene Turner's address, and they began corresponding. Lorene was an orphan and was like a sister to Geri. In fact, Geri's parents called her their girl, and she was very special. Everyone who knew her loved her and felt that she deserved the very best. When Gus received the Holy Ghost, I felt like he was the best! It certainly proved true to those who knew him. Lorene writes, "We were married on January 11, 1954, and Gus was discharged from the air force on September 27, 1954. He enrolled in Apostolic Bible Institute in the spring of 1955. Brother A. T. Morgan, then general superintendent of the United Pentecostal Church, signed his ministerial license on June 19, 1958, and we began evangelizing immediately. He was promoted to Heaven on May 31, 2003."

I was best man at the wedding and Geri was matron of honor as my brother George performed the ceremony. Once my family met Gus, they adopted him and considered him one of the family. He was a tremendous preacher and could draw a word picture better than anyone I ever knew. When he "shot the arrow," it went straight to the target! I will add that after I came home, I found myself in trouble with several of the girls in the church in DeRidder for not giving their addresses to an airman.

God is amazing! How He brings things together is a wonder to behold! As I have previously mentioned, Gus and I volunteered on the same day and arrived at Lackland AFB the same day on the same train. We left on buses a week later for Shepherd AFB and later met at Camp Stoneman. From there we went to Okinawa, where Gus received the Holy Ghost.

The Lord works in mysterious ways. Kenneth Field's company was sent to Korea, but for some unknown reason he and one other man, Archie (his last name escapes me now), were sent to Okinawa. Every man in his original company was killed in Korea! I met him the first Saturday evening of September when I preached at Youth for Christ. When Kenneth received the

Holy Ghost, he went back to his barracks, entered, threw up his hands, and shouted as loud as he could, "I just received the Holy Ghost!" Nobody objected and they all listened. The next week, Archie came with him, and he received the Holy Ghost. Kenneth would bring someone with him almost every service. When he rotated back to the States, he was discharged and went to his home in Arizona. There he began attending a United Pentecostal church pastored by Brother Green. Brother Green had a daughter, and Kenneth started dating her. They were soon married and made a wonderful team. He won his brother to the Lord, and that man now is the district superintendent of the South Dakota District of the United Pentecostal Church International. Kenneth became youth president of the Arizona District, then later moved to Oxnard, California, where he built a powerful church, which he pastored the rest of his life. Over twenty-five ministers came from that church, and he was responsible for many more. He called me in 2002 to preach an anniversary service for him. Then, less than a year later, he called me again, saying he had a request to make of me. "I want you to preach my funeral." That shocked me! He then said that he had cancer, and the doctors only gave him a few weeks to live. He said he had been feeling bad for some time and finally went to the doctor for a checkup. They discovered the cancer in the last stages. He was only concerned about his lovely wife. He said, "I'm ready, and if God wants to take me, I'm ready and happy to go." His funeral was a victorious one. I told of our meeting in Okinawa, and the people worshiped and praised the Lord. It is so wonderful to know that you are ready to go!

Me baptizing Kenneth Fields

Walking to the China Sea to baptize Kenneth Fields
Left to right: Jack Deadwyler, Kenneth, me, Tom Gordan, and
John Goodman

His father-in-law, Brother Green, was an amazing man who
loved to debate other denominations about this truth. At one

debate the preacher began to belittle him and his church about their lack of education. For most of his opening speech, he continued to belittle him and his church. When Brother Green took the floor, he said, "Folks, I came here to debate, and this gentleman has done nothing but run my church down about our lack of education. I grant you I have only a tenth-grade education as I had to drop out of school to go to work to help support my family. I wish I had the education he has, but I was never able to continue in school. But I will tell you what I will do; for every Scripture he can quote, I will give him a hundred dollars if I can't quote the Scripture before it and the one after it." Needless to say, he kept all his money and it cost him nothing.

Most of our success in Okinawa came as a result of preaching at the Youth for Christ. It seemed to me that I was loved by a few and hated by many. Some were continually trying to have me preach again at YFC. They did have me preach on the Armed Forces Radio Network, which reached half the world. The two messages were taped, and I was told later that they used those tapes every three or four months. A chaplain was scheduled to preach one Saturday night and he didn't show up. When it came time for the preacher and he was not there, the audience insisted the leader ask me to speak. It was quite comical; I was halfway through the message when the chaplain walked in. From the back of the chapel the leader motioned for me to sit and let the chaplain take over, and I refused. I went on and finished my message, with them continually motioning for me to stop. I finished and sat down, and the chaplain took the pulpit. He was Episcopal and proceeded to give everyone a tongue-lashing for not being Episcopal. Many in the congregation came to me later and thanked me for the message, apologizing for the raving and ranting of the chaplain. I had never heard a chaplain do as he did. Who knows? Maybe the ten minutes he listened to me disturbed his thinking.

A civilian worker on the island, Helen Ressler, was one of the leaders in Youth for Christ. She was beyond the age of the youth group, but age made no difference because the leadership needed all the help they could get. We never talked or witnessed to her as she kept herself out of reach of any of our group. We went to the Youth for Christ meeting every Saturday evening even though the leadership was not happy to have us. After I preached there, they tried to distance themselves from me. Still, there were a number who respected me and wanted to have me preach again.

A few days after a preaching service, Helen approached Gus, wanting to talk, and he brought her to my office. She began to cry and said, "My world has caved in on me! I realize now that I do not have what God has for me. I have watched you and see that you have something I don't have, and I need it."

We began talking about this wonderful Holy Ghost experience, and she said, "I want the Holy Ghost, and I want you to baptize me."

I had found the perfect place to baptize. Before that we had to walk a hundred yards into the China Sea and then have the seeker kneel to be baptized because the water was so shallow. We found a landing barge they used in WWII that was stuck in the sand on the shore. The waves had continued to hit it and had washed out a deep hole. We baptized her in Jesus' name, and she received the Holy Ghost shortly after.

She was a great blessing to us as she had a vehicle and would either go with us or allow us to use her vehicle to go to our Bible classes. I taught as many Bible classes as I could, but we were conducting fourteen classes over the island and were forced to use those who had recently prayed through. We were on an island; we couldn't go anywhere and thus had a lot of time for teaching. Helen's boyfriend would not go along with us, and after a while they broke up. She continued to work for Youth for Christ even though they didn't like her association with us.

After Gus and I were rotated home, she remained there for at least a year, working with the Okinawans. She then returned home and enrolled in Apostolic Bible Institute. After graduating she remained in St. Paul, working in the church there. Then she moved to Bellflower, California. I heard later that she was taking care of a mobile home for a family while they were on vacation, when someone broke in and killed her. She was a marvelous Christian, a brilliant person, and a tremendous worker for the kingdom of God.

John Concesico, Helen Ressler, and two others I baptized

The chaplains would not give us a place to have service. The first place we found was a tomb. The Okinawans buried their dead in tombs, and in WWII the doors were blown off a number of them. We found one that was clean and large enough, so we went in and had our service. We moved in a few weeks to a chapel a Baptist chaplain allowed us to use. Pressure was applied to him, so after two weeks we were forced to move. This happened two or three times. Finally we located a deserted chapel in the "boondocks" that had been closed for a couple of years. We crawled through the window and had service. Then someone broke the lock off the door, and we could go in the front door. We cleaned it up and painted the windows black to shield the light from the outside.

Our deserted chapel where we had church

There we met every Monday night, and often we would go there to pray through the week. Gus and Kenneth received the Holy Ghost there, plus a number of others. We used this chapel about four months, and then one Monday, after concluding our service, I said to the group, "As of tonight, we are no longer using this building." It shocked them, and they asked why. I answered, "I don't know. I just know that when we walk out tonight we are no longer using this chapel."

The next day the wing chaplain came to me and asked, "Glass, are you using that chapel on the hill?"

I said, "No, sir, I am not."

"I know you are using that chapel, and I am going to have you court-martialed for trespassing on government property."

"But, Chaplain, I am not using that chapel," I said.

He went away in a rage, not able to do a thing to me. If he would have said, "You have been using that chapel," I would have said, "Yes, sir." But I told the group the night before we would no longer use this chapel. God knew how I would say it, and He caused the chaplain to say just what he said. God works in mysterious ways.

We continued to have problems finding a place to have services on Okinawa and decided to go to Naha, a city nearby. We approached the pastor of the chapel where the Youth for Christ group held services every Saturday. He consented, and for three weeks we were there. Then pressure was put on the pastor, and we had to move. One in our group went to the Congress of the Ryukyu Islands (one thousand islands off the southern tip of Japan, Okinawa being the capital island). They seemed surprised to see an American come before them and asked what he wanted. He answered, "We want a place to have church each Monday night. Could you help us?"

They answered, "Here's our congressional building. You may use it."

For the next fourteen months we used their building. A janitor let us in, and we had overstuffed chairs, plush carpet, and a well-lit room with clean floors. They put the town "off limits" occasionally, but we would go to our CO and get a pass to go to church. The chaplains tried to find out where we were meeting and we never tried to hide it, yet they never found out.

During this time, I taught a class at an army post called Camp Kue. The chaplain allowed us to use it once a week. That lasted for three months. One night I went to service and found a note on the pulpit saying, "I don't understand it, but I have orders to not let you use this chapel any longer. I am sorry." I then heard of a church in a small village not far from Camp Kue.

The pastor had gone to Japan, so I approached his sisters about using the church. They gave me permission. The building was only about twenty by forty feet, very small by our standards. We started services there, and the first service the building was so packed that I only had a space of maybe three feet for me and my interpreter to stand. It was that way every service.

Brother Tokeshi with two of his helpers

When the pastor, Brother Tokeshi, came home, he was overjoyed to see so many people, but he had heard about our teachings and was somewhat troubled, not understanding the doctrine. He was reluctant to talk to me about this and went back to Japan to try to straighten out his thinking. The first place he went to was Brother Jan Mauri's Bible school, which was in fellowship with the United Pentecostal Church. After Brother Mauri explained the message to him, he accepted it and was baptized in Jesus' name and received the Holy Ghost. Although I paid tithes to my home church, we all paid tithes to our work in Okinawa, and we began supporting Brother Tokeshi and his ministry. We were also allowed to have Bible classes in different schools at this time.

When I was on leave preparing to go overseas, my father was taken to the hospital with gangrene in his left foot. After an examination, they informed the family that they would have to remove his left leg above the knee. I arrived home just in time to help hold him on the operating table while they gave him a spinal shot for the surgery. He had been in such pain for so long that as soon as the shot took effect, he went to sleep. After the surgery we took him to a room because in that hospital they had no intensive care. The family was with him, and the doctor told us he would die at any moment as it was impossible for him to live. The poison had gone throughout his body, but we continued to pray. We heard Dad give a loud gasp and quit breathing. We watched as the nurse picked up his railroad watch and got the time, and then she took the sheet to put over his head. I fell across a chair, and we all began to cry out to God for mercy. How could we ask for mercy since God had shown us so much mercy? Before the nurse could drop the sheet over Dad's face, there was another loud gasp and Dad started breathing again. The nurse was so startled she leaped to her feet and ran for the doctor. Three doctors and several nurses came in and dismissed us as they checked on Dad. After a while the head nurse, who had been Dad's assistant when he was health inspector, came to us, and we were all smiling. "We don't know what happened in there, but don't get your hopes up. There is still no way he can live. He will be gone at any minute." We just smiled and thanked her, and she went away disgusted at us for not believing her.

The family left the hospital and went home to get some rest while I stayed with Dad. I stayed until eight the next morning, and he continued to breathe normally. Dad went home five days later. Two months later he was back on his job as health inspector for Beauregard Parish. Several months later he went for a checkup, and the doctor told him he could go back to work in another month. Dad chuckled and said, "I've been working for a month."

He wasn't home but a few days when he wanted to go to church but was told there was no way anyone could get him up the stairs to the auditorium. He said, "Just drive the car to the side door and leave the church door open; I will be able to hear the service."

When they drove up to the church, four men simply picked up the wheelchair and carried him to the auditorium. When the altar call was given, Dad rolled himself to the altar, where he prayed through. After that he insisted on being in service every time the church doors opened. There was such a tremendous difference in his life! One day, one of his old friends came to see him, and Dad said to him, "I was in the hospital, my family gave me up, and I died."

Lucille heard him and said, "That's not true, Dad. We never gave you up, and you didn't die."

He said to her, "Daughter, don't tell me I didn't die! My feet were already in the fire when a hand reached down and lifted me out. A voice said, 'Bob, I'm giving you one more chance.'"

Then on July 12, 1952 (July 13 on Okinawa), Dad had gone to church with Mother, Lucille, Larry, Charles, and Mary Jo. After the service, they came home and were sitting at the table eating when Dad got up, walked a few steps with his crutches into the hall, and fell to the floor. Lucille ran to get a wet cloth and prayed, "O Lord, don't let him die."

Then the Lord spoke to her and said, "Daughter, you asked Me to let him live then because he wasn't ready. He is ready now!"

She cried out, "O Lord, have Your own way."

When she went to bathe his face, he opened his eyes brightly and cried out, "I've been in the presence of the Lord! Not my will, Lord, but Thine be done." So God took him at that moment. What a wonderful and merciful Savior!

On July 13, 1952, I received a radio phone call from home. I had to go to a special place on the island to answer it. (This was a long time before satellites.) I was informed that my father had died two hours earlier. This was a hard blow to me. Brother Wellborn, a family friend, told me that they were going to request that I come home for the funeral. It was a hard thing for me to say, but I told them that I could not leave. They insisted, but I felt that if I ever left, I would never come back. The air force would reassign me to the States. The work was such that all might be lost if I should leave.

After receiving the phone call, I went to the wing chaplain's office and told him my father had just passed away. He said very tenderly, "Sit down. I do this for the others; let me talk to you." He read John 14:1-3, "Let not your heart be troubled: ye believe in God, believe also in me. In my Father's house are many mansions: if it were not so, I would have told you. I go to prepare a place for you. And if I go and prepare a place for you, I will come again, and receive you unto myself; that where I am, there ye may be also." He then commented on these verses, and they were a great comfort to me. Since then, I have used this passage in almost every funeral I have conducted.

After I turned down the trip home for the funeral, the work there exploded. I had fourteen Bible studies every week with the Okinawans. We used our tithes to send the first four Okinawan ladies I baptized to Japan to Brother Coots' Bible college. I soon took a leave and went to Japan to see Brother Coots, and it didn't cost me anything to fly because I took a "hop"—terminology for catching a military plane that was going there anyway. I wanted to check out the college because I had heard so many bad things about it. I was glad to find that none of it was true and that it was an excellent college. I spent an entire week there and enjoyed it very much. We paid for the ladies' transportation, gave them some money to get settled in the school, and were able to send them some money each month. Brother Coots agreed to take care of most of their expenses and later wrote of the students: "And I just wish that some of the folks who were not fully in favor of building the Bible college could have been with us at the New Year's convention of 1954. The Okinawan contingent of seven girls broke down, wept as if their hearts would break as they pled with God for a mighty visitation of the Spirit upon their island. I promised that, in God's time, I would definitely seek to go there and bring a moving of the Spirit up Okinawa." I am sure he was talking about the seven girls and the one man I sent to his college. Later we sent four more students: three girls and a boy.

The four Okinawan ladies I baptized
and sent to Japan for Bible college

Bible college students

Me prepairing to eat with the Okinawans at the baptism

Brother Tokeshi and some of the 125 we batized

Brother Tokeshi baptized around five hundred people in one week in November 1952. Easter Sunday 1953 he and I went to the Kadena River, and with about five hundred in attendance at the all-day service, we baptized 125. They were planning to eat there, too—what we called in the States "dinner on the ground." Gus and other airmen who had received the Holy Ghost were there. After the baptismal service and before the meal, I turned to Gus and John and said, "Let's go."

John said, "Go? What do you want to go for?"

"Let's go," I said again, but we had waited too late. The church member came, took me by the arm, and led me to the center of the crowd, where they handed me a paper with a large ball of rice with fish heads in it. Then they had a lady pray for the food, and she prayed an anointed prayer although I couldn't understand much of it. I was in some distress over being expected to eat the rice ball. They wouldn't take a bite until I did. So I bravely put it to my mouth and took a bite. Everyone followed. I turned, and John was eating it like it was the best food in the world. I felt as if I should have made him eat mine also. I soon bid everyone good-bye, and we walked back to our vehicle. When I got out of sight of the crowd, I closed the paper around the food and threw it as far as I could.

After WWII as the United States began rebuilding Okinawa, the Methodist missionary and the chaplains got together with the Christians. There were five Christian groups on the island—American Baptist, Methodist, Disciples of Christ, Presbyterian, and a Holiness group. They banded together and sought to keep "denominations" out of Okinawa. The president of the association, Rev. Higa, had written a commentary on the New Testament in the Okinawan language. (They spoke Japanese with a different dialect.) Rev. Higa had sent me word that he would like to talk to me. I was certainly looking forward to it, but when the American chaplains and the Methodist missionary heard of our meeting, they went to him and said, "If you talk to Glass, we will withdraw all of our support from you and your pastors. We will quit rebuilding your churches." Because of this I was notified that there would be no meeting. Some members of his board were faithful to attend our Bible classes, and they told those of their association who attended that I should baptize them in the name of Jesus Christ.

Christmas was approaching, and I wanted to get some candy and fruit for the children who attended our services. I mentioned this to Gus and the others, and Gus said, "There are better ways we can spend our money." I tried to explain to Gus that this was a good idea, but he just couldn't see it. Then one in our group went to the dining hall, and the mess sergeant gave us a few crates of oranges and apples. Jack Deadwyler, who had rotated back to the States, wrote and said he was sending fifty pounds of candy. Gus helped us sack it and on Christmas Eve helped give it to the kids. Afterward, he came to me with tears in his eyes and said, "Arless, I understand now. This is wonderful! Look how happy they are with this little bit we are giving." Gus was wonderful! What a tremendous soulwinner and blessing he was to me and everyone. I had no brother any closer to me.

We visited the leper colony on an island just off the coast of Okinawa. There were 999 lepers on the island. A young man who was a schoolteacher and one of our interpreters went with us. He had received the Holy Ghost and we had baptized him. We conducted a service there, and this young man became so burdened for the lepers that he dedicated his life to teaching them. Another interpreter had received the Holy Ghost and was baptized and worked with us for over a year. He left us and went to work for the Okinawa government. He later became the liaison between Okinawa, Japan, and the United States.

A woman caring for a child at the leper colony

The colony's laundry room

The school building in the leper colony
where we taught Bible classes

Children in the leper colony are only allowed
to see their parents a few miniutes a day
with no physical contact

A teacher I baptized who dedicated his life
to teaching in the colony

I could say a lot about the opposition, of which I had plenty, but I felt that it only went with the territory. I was assigned to the 6332nd Wing, 20th Air Force as permanent party on Kadena AFB. On the base were two bombardment wings, the 307th and the 19th. They were both on temporary duty on the island; their permanent bases were in the States. They were assigned to the island for a period of six months with their B-29s bombing Korea almost every day. After six months the men were rotated back to the States.

I was assigned to the chaplain of the 307th on temporary duty from my wing. I lived in a "tent city" without all the conveniences that my permanent wing was enjoying. I had been there about three months when I baptized the 6332nd wing chaplain's assistant and he received the Holy Ghost. He was so overjoyed that he had to tell it. That brought the wrath of the wing chaplain on me.

He then visited our 307th chapel and told me, "I'm going to pull you away from this chapel and put you with me, and I will bust you!"

I went to Chaplain Hurley and said, "Sir, they are pulling me away from you and back to my permanent wing."

He said, "I know; you will get your orders today. I am sorry to lose you. What do they have against you anyway?"

I answered, "They strongly oppose what I preach. I preach that baptism is essential for salvation."

He jumped to his feet and said, "Heavens to Betsy! Don't those fools know that our blessed Lord said, 'Except a man be born of water and of the Spirit, he cannot enter into the kingdom of God'? He also said, 'He that believeth and is baptized shall be saved.' What is wrong with them? Don't they know the Bible? Don't worry! I'm going to force them to leave you here."

He went to the orderly room and into the CO's office and said to him, "They are taking Sergeant Glass from me today."

"Yes. He's under orders to leave today."

The chaplain asked, "How many men do they have on temporary duty from us?"

The CO answered, "Fourteen."

The chaplain said, "Inform them we are pulling all our men from them if they take Sergeant Glass."

He called, and the orders were cancelled. I remained with the 307th for another three months. During that time the wing chaplain was moved to another chapel, and someone else took his place. Later, I went back to wing as NCOIC (Non-Commissioned Officer In Charge) over all the chapels on Kadena AFB.

Chaplain Hurley had been on Okinawa for a year and was supposed to rotate in six months. He was notified one day that if he could be ready in twenty-four hours, he could go back to the States. He began the work of preparing to go home. Two hours before he was to leave, two officers came to the office to take him to the flight line. The chaplain opened his cabinet door, and there were four full bottles of liquor. He said, "I won't need these any more"; so he gave two each to the two officers.

As he was preparing to walk out the door, the two officers went to their knees and said, "Father, bless me!"

Chaplain Hurley turned to bless them, paused a moment and said, "Bless you with a quart of liquor in each hand? Oh, well." He made the sign of the cross, touched their foreheads, and pronounced a blessing on them.

Eight people we baptized

Completing a baptismal service

Four more we baptized

John Goodman beside me and six Okinawans we baptized

Yohama, our interpreter who received the Holy Ghost and later became the liaison between the U.S. forces and Japan

Me teaching in one of my classes

One day I received an order to report to the general of the army who was in charge of the military operations on Okinawa.

I walked into his office, saluted, and stood at attention. He said, "At ease, Sergeant."

He informed me that all the chaplains and missionaries on Okinawa were very disturbed by my preaching. He said that I was causing much disturbance among the military personnel and the civilian population of Okinawa. He then proceeded to tell me that he was ordering me to cease my preaching and that I was not to speak to anyone else concerning my beliefs. I was to keep it to myself, and if I continued, he would arrest me, put me in the stockade, and court-martial me.

"Sir, will that be a written order?" I asked.

He answered, "It is a verbal order, and you obey it."

I said, "Sir, if you put it in writing, I will consider it."

He shouted, "It is a verbal order, and you will obey it."

I then said, "Sir, I will not obey it! This is American soil, and I have my freedoms that neither you nor anyone else can take from me. I lost two brothers in WWII, and another two served, one in France and the other as a guerrilla fighter behind the Japanese lines in China. Two served and two died so that I could have the freedom to preach according to the dictates of my conscience, and neither you nor anyone else will take that freedom from me!"

He then informed me that he would have me arrested for not obeying an order. I restated that I would not obey, and then he ordered me to leave. I went back to my quarters, got my material, went into the village, and taught a Bible lesson. I never heard from the general again.

One of the missionaries went into a village and had the school president call a special assembly. He then preached to them a sermon on John 3:16, "For God so loved the world, that he gave his only begotten Son, that whosoever believeth in him should not perish, but have everlasting life." After his sermon he asked the student body, "How many of you believe on Jesus Christ? Raise your hand." The people would do anything asked of them, and they all raised their hands. Then he asked them, "How many of you will accept Him as your personal Savior? Raise your hand." They all raised their hands.

He then sent me a message saying, "You can come into this village and sow your damnable doctrine now, and it won't hurt anyone. I have gotten them all saved, and nothing you can say or do will destroy them."

I read the article he sent to his church magazine that stated, "I went to a certain village, preached at a school, and had six hundred receive Christ as their personal Savior."

Behind the main chapel was a house where three of the chaplains lived. One of the chaplains came into our office complex laughing. He had to tell his story and said, "Boy, have we played a trick on the wing chaplain! We slipped into his room and found his liquor; the bottle was about half full. We drank that and then filled it with tea. Is he going to be surprised?"

As NCOIC without an order from the chaplains, I could use what I wished for communion and always used grape juice. However, I had to keep a supply of wine on hand for any chaplain who wished to use it. So I ordered a case of wine, and the wing chaplain said to me, "Let's store that in my office, where it will be safe."

Later, I went to take inventory of the wine. The chaplain was sitting at his desk when I shouted, "Chaplain, I'm missing four bottles of wine!"

He said, "Ha-ha, I wonder what could have happened to it?" Then he chuckled again.

Later, the chaplains got together and chose one of them to talk to me, to show me the error of my ways. An army chaplain, a Nazarene who had twelve years of college and seminary, was chosen. I was ordered to report to him in his quarters. When I arrived, he greeted me warmly and seemed to have a very pleasing personality. We began talking, and he mentioned the problems I was causing and asked if there was a way it could be prevented.

He began explaining his Trinity doctrine to me and the plan of salvation as he taught it. He also said that they really would like to keep denominations out of Okinawa and have everyone preach the same doctrine. They really would be happy for me to continue preaching if I preached the same message as they did.

Finally I said to him, "Chaplain, if you were man enough to admit it, you believe like I do, but you are not man enough to admit it."

He said, "Sergeant, I would never believe like you."

I then said, "You believe in three persons in the Godhead, the Father—one person, the Son—second person, the Holy Ghost—third person."

He answered, "Yes, and you believe in only one."

I said, "That's right." I took three objects, put them down, and said, "One, two, three."

He then took two of them, stacked them on top of one, and said, "No, there's just one."

I said to him, "That's how I believe, and that One's name is Jesus."

He said, "No, no, there are three persons in the Godhead."

I then put the three objects down again and counted, "One, two, three."

He again said, "No, there's only one!"

I again said, "And His name is Jesus."

We went through that a couple more times, and then he said, "You're impossible! You may go!" I believe I may have shaken him up a bit and never heard from him again.

The chaplains got together again to decide what to do with me. They talked about sending me to Japan, a three-year tour of duty. One chaplain spoke up and said, "They will have the same trouble with him there." Another suggested they transfer me out of the chaplaincy and to a line job. One said, "With him here we know what he's doing; away from here we wouldn't know." So I stayed where I was.

After my father died I applied for an allotment for my mother. When the allotment was approved, I was notified by my orderly room that if I had sufficient papers to submit, it would cut my tour of duty down to eighteen months. That was the length of duty for a man with dependents. That would mean I would go home in January instead of the next June. I paid fifty dollars to call home to tell my fiancee, Geri Gill, what I needed and that our pastor, George Glass, could get it for me. (Why didn't I call my pastor? You're kidding!) I waited for a couple of weeks, and the papers arrived. When I read them, they were not what I asked for at all. I took them to the man in charge, and he rejected them.

I called home again and said, "I told you what I needed, and you didn't send me the proper papers."

Geri replied, "Well, I told Brother Glass what you said, and he said that wasn't what I needed and that he would get the papers I needed."

I was a little perturbed at that and said, "What does he know about the air force? They require the very papers I asked for."

She had them done over, sent them, and they arrived three days after a new directive came from Washington that stated a person with dependents must stay full term. God was in this!

I had informed the wing chaplain that I would be going home six months early. He said, "That's good. I think it is only right for them to send you home early." He sounded so relieved; however, it was short-lived. "I will appoint a replacement for you to train," he said. He then canceled the transfer to Japan they were working on. A few weeks later he asked me when I was going home. I replied that there was a new directive and that I would have to stay another six months. He shouted, "That's not fair! They shouldn't do this to you." I smiled because I knew of his former plans. Someone always kept me informed as to what they were doing. He then contacted the chaplains and said that they would have to go on with the transfer. He then called the orderly room and told them to go through with the transfer to Japan. (They had planned to send me to the worst base in Japan.) The first sergeant informed him that a transfer for me was impossible. The reason: I was to be rotated home in six months, and my name had already been submitted to Washington for rotation. I must remain on base until my rotation date was due. What a shock to them! I was happy with this situation. So, to save face, the wing chaplain decided to transfer me three months later to the Flight Line Chapel, which was the 19th Bombardment Group. I would be working with the chaplain who had said he was going to "bust" me.

This chaplain, McClelland from Arkansas, did not try to convert me; he just took me under his arm as if I were his own son and began teaching me things about the ministry. We became good friends. He wanted me with him everywhere he went and treated me royally. I got to the office early and made the coffee every morning. One morning he said to me, "Sergeant Glass, let's learn to drink coffee without sugar and cream." I agreed and tried it for two weeks and couldn't take it any longer. I went back to putting sugar in my coffee. About a week later he spoke loudly, "Bring me some sugar; I can't stand this any longer." I told him that I had started using sugar a week ago. He then asked why I didn't tell him.

The living conditions were great in this assignment. I moved into a brand-new building, private room, and mess hall for NCOs only. It was the best food I had during my entire enlistment. I walked into the mess hall one morning for breakfast, and they were celebrating the three hundredth bomb run over Korea. To celebrate, they flew in fresh eggs from the Philippines. I cannot tell you how good those eggs tasted! We all wanted seconds but had to be satisfied with the two given us. They soon opened a state-side restaurant in front of our barracks. I went to the restaurant and saw something I hadn't seen since leaving home—a double-dip ice cream cone. I bought one and walked outside to eat it. Everyone who passed paused to look, and almost all of them had to go in and buy one, too.

In the midst of all the opposition, one day I was in the jeep in the boondocks with the wing chaplain. He pulled up to a stop sign, turned to me, and said, "We are not as dumb as you think we are."

I was surprised at these words and asked, "What do you mean, Chaplain?"

He answered, "We know more about the Bible than you think we know. We know what you teach! We know that the Bible doesn't teach a Trinity. Give us a man who can use the Bible and prove a Trinity, and we will make him a millionaire. We get the Trinity from only two places in the Bible. One is where Jesus said I come from the Father, I go to the Father, and I will send another. The other place is Matthew 28:19, where Jesus said to baptize in the name of the Father, the Son, and the Holy Ghost. We also know that He never said those words. They were added later. Jesus said, 'In my name.' But the Trinity is a mystery and is ritual. The people love ritual, and we are going to give them what they want." He then put the jeep in gear and drove off without another word.

Another chaplain called me to his office one day and said, "I have an article I want you to read." It was written by F. F. Bruce, Hebrew and Greek professor at the Baptist Seminary in New Orleans, Louisiana, and entitled "Jesus the Mighty God." I read it and almost shouted. He said, "That's a good article, isn't it?" He proceeded to preach a Oneness sermon. I sat there amazed and thrilled. Then he said to me, "Of course, I don't believe that article or what I have just said to you. I am a Baptist and am not allowed to believe it." I asked for that article, but he would not part with it.

During this time, I lived in a room in back of the chapel. The three chaplains lived in a house about fifty feet away. My walls were constructed of wood four feet up and then wire screen to the ceiling. There were shutters over the wire that could be closed, but I never did because it was so hot. I was somewhat isolated from the others and halfway expected someone would stick a gun through the screen some night and shoot me. We don't want to think that religious opposition can get so bad, but believe me it can! I never lost any sleep over it because I knew I was there in the will of God and He was going to take care of me.

Considering how much opposition I had on Okinawa, it is amazing how God took care of me! I had been in the air force for only ten weeks when I was recommended for my first stripe PFC. Two weeks later I was recommended for corporal. When the CO got my paperwork for that promotion, he sent it back. He wrote this note. "This man has a total of two months and twenty eight days in service with six days in grade as PFC. Since it took the good Lord seven days and seven nights to create the heavens and the earth, I suggest His helpers spend at least twice that time in grade!" My office just retyped the request and sent it in, and I was given my second stripe. The Catholic chaplain got me my third stripe with only eleven months in service, and it was supposed to take thirty-five months. Then the wing chaplain said, "Put everyone in for promotion." I was put in for my fourth stripe, staff sergeant, after I had only nineteen months in service and eight months in grade. It usually takes fifty-five months to make the grade of staff sergeant, but I made it in less than twenty months.

The master sergeant on the promotion board asked me, "How have you made rank so fast?"

I answered, "I don't know. Maybe it's because of my qualifications. I'm a licensed preacher."

He then said, "You mean you preach sermons?"

The wing chaplain had told me beforehand, "You will be a mighty good man if you make this promotion." When I told him that I had made it, he said, "They told me you couldn't possibly make it." This was just another blessing from the Lord!

After I had volunteered for the air force, I applied for a local license. The board met in February 1951. I was prepared to meet the board, but because of an ice storm, it was impossible to get there. A few weeks later I received my license in the mail. The license certainly helped me in the service when I had to prove a number of times that I was qualified for the ministry. The 20th Air Force chaplain called me in one day and said that I could not preach on the island because I was not qualified. I then showed him my license, and without another word he dismissed me. After coming home, my brother George put me in for ordination. At the Louisiana camp meeting I met the board, and they only asked me about the work in Okinawa. I was ordained at that camp meeting. Many have asked me what it is like to meet the board for license, and I tell them they'll have to ask someone else because I never did that.

When I had been on Okinawa for fifteen months, I went into the orderly room, sat at the desk of the first sergeant, and said, "I want a transfer!"

"Where do you want to go?" he asked.

"I want to go home!"

"Don't give me that, Glass! Your name is on the general's desk as the man with the highest morale on this island!"

That was the end of that. It is amazing how we are watched when we know nothing about it. I was happy, and God blessed me every way I turned.

Years later, after we came home, Gus said to me, "Arless, you showed such great faith on Okinawa. The many impossible places you were in, the heavy opposition you had, but God brought you out of it all." I answered that I didn't think that was anything unusual as it was just going from day to day and trusting God to take care of our needs.

I could relate many other experiences I had on the Island of Okinawa. While I was on temporary duty and living in a tent, at two o'clock one morning someone began rolling up the tent next to where I was sleeping. The man who rolled it up said to me, "Arless, you've got to come pray with me! I've got to have the Holy Ghost!" I dressed, went with him into the tall weeds away from the tent area, and prayed with him for about fifteen minutes until he started speaking in tongues.

Another time I met a master sergeant named Jack Deadwyler, an air policeman and an African-American. We talked and he later came to one of our services. During the altar service I laid hands on him, and he started speaking in tongues. He fell to the floor and for a long time praised God and spoke in tongues. I later baptized him in the China Sea, and from that day at every baptismal service he would say, "In Jesus' name! Brother Arless, baptize me again." Many days when I finished my day's work and went to my quarters, he would be there waiting for me and would say, "Brother Arless, let's go and send up timbers for Heaven!" We would go to the deserted chapel and pray. Before he was to rotate home, another African American airman, Sergeant John D. Goodman, came to service and received the Holy Ghost. Then another, John Concesico, came and was also filled. When I left Okinawa, I turned the work to Brother Concesico. Brother Deadwyler came home, and after his discharge, he started a church in Peoria, Illinois. He built it with his own money and also started an organization, preaching the same message as the United Pentecostal Church. In 1980 I was told there were thirty-six churches in that organization, the largest running over three thousand members.

One night six of us were coming home from our Monday night service in a jeep. One in the group became sick, and we began to pray. One who had not yet received the Holy Ghost said, "Look, all you have to do is believe, and healing is yours." Then he said, "Wow! Glory!" and started speaking in tongues, and we all began shouting and praising God. As we came to the gate of the base, he continued speaking with tongues, and I said to the others, "Start laughing!" We did and drove through the gate as we left the guard scratching his head, wondering what was going on.

I baptized twin brothers, Troy and Toy, and they received the Holy Ghost. I cannot remember their last name. I studied them for a long time and finally said, "You're Toy." He said, "No, I'm Troy." So I gave up on telling them apart.

When I was in the good graces of the wing chaplain, he tried his best to get me to have Geri come over and let him marry us, and have us remain there for the rest of my tour of duty. Should I have done that, it would have been very difficult to leave the island.

To God be the glory!

HOME AGAIN

I remember that after I received my orders to come home, I would wave them to the other airmen and say, "Boys, I got my parole today." We called Okinawa "The Rock," after Alcatraz, and it was not the favorite duty assignment. I know that as the years pass, we tend to remember the good times and forget the bad experiences. I know I had some bad times, but the good times so far outweighed the bad that the memories of my time on Okinawa are mostly good ones. Since Gus was scheduled to go home in a couple of weeks and Kenneth Fields was already in the States, I appointed John Concesico and Helen Ressler to take over the classes I was teaching.

When I was ready to ship out, they gave me three choices of transportation. One was a ship going to Korea for two days, then to the Philippines for two days, and then on to Hawaii for two days. The second was a plane trip that would go around the world, from Okinawa to Japan to Singapore, to Europe and England, and on to the United States. The third was a ship that would go for one day to Japan and then on to the United States, and this ship was to take thirteen days. I said, "Give me that one," as it sounded like the shortest time and I wanted to get home as quickly as possible. Now, I wish I had taken the plane ride around the world, but I just wanted to get home!

I left Okinawa in May 1953, arriving home that month. When I boarded the ship, the *USS Randall*, I watched as a group of Okinawans gathered on the dock. They searched until they saw me in the crowd at the rail. I was waving to them, and when they saw me and the ship started to move, sounding its horn, Brother Tokeshi held up one finger, then eight fingers, then five fingers. I understood that it was page 185 in their songbook, "When We All Get to Heaven." Then they began to sing. What a sendoff that was! I stood and watched with tears in my eyes until they were out of sight.

Staging area before leaving Okinawa

Okinawans at the dock to see me off, singing
"When We All Get to Heaven"

Arriving in San Francisco with the band playing

I sought for Brother Stairs, the Foreign Missions director, to come over to organize the work, but for some reason he never came. They were ready for it and were asking for help. Since the UPC never acted, Brother Tokeshi contacted Brother Mauri, who sent ten couples to take over the work. The report I received in 1960 was that over twelve thousand had been baptized in Jesus' name and received the Holy Ghost. I was sorry that the UPC did not go but very happy that they were preaching the same message. I only know that Brother Coots had promised to go to Okinawa. If it was in his power, he did so. I do know that the students returned and continued in the work of God.

When the ship arrived in Japan, they gave everyone shore leave for an entire day. I was not interested in going ashore, so I stayed on the ship. One of the airmen asked if he could borrow my belt as his was packed and he couldn't find it. I did so, and after they left an officer saw me and started to reprimand me for being out of uniform. I explained to him what I had done, and to my pleasant surprise, he let it drop.

The trip that was supposed to take thirteen days took only eleven. They told us they were going to break the record, and they did. My job on the ship was to guard four prisoners. They were four Jehovah's Witnesses who, the chaplains explained, had gotten "mail-order religion." They joined the church and then informed the officers that as of a certain date they would not sound the alarm if the enemy were attacking. Since they were assigned to a radar unit, this was considered refusing to do their duty. Their church would not allow them to take part in any war. They were tried by court martial, found guilty, and sentenced to six years in federal prison. I talked to them, trying to show them the truth of God, but they were completely brainwashed. Nothing I could say would sway them from their belief.

When we arrived in San Francisco harbor, other airmen relieved me of my duty, and we boarded buses for Parks AFB, where we were to be debriefed and then sent home. On my first day at Parks, I went for breakfast at the mess hall. Those on the serving line were all basic trainees. When one gave me a half-pint of milk, I asked for more since I had only drunk powdered milk for two years. He said he was only allowed to give me one.

I said firmly, "I want another!"

"Yes, sir," he answered and gave me another.

You cannot imagine how good that milk tasted! It was real milk! When I was growing up, I would not drink anything but raw milk. Now, I don't like raw milk at all but must have homogenized.

We were told that we must have a haircut before we would be allowed to leave for home. The day before I left Okinawa, I went to the barber shop and told the barber I was going home the next day. He spent over an hour giving me the best haircut I ever had. Afraid that they might not let me go unless I got another one, I ran to the barber shop ahead of a hundred others and still had to wait over an hour. I told the barber that I was going home to get married and wanted a good haircut. He asked me something I'd never heard before, "What will you give me for a good haircut?" I really didn't know how to take that, so I just said, "I want a haircut." This made him mad, and he gave me the worst haircut I had ever had.

They informed us that all airlines were completely full and it may take two or three days to get out. I had already bought a first-class ticket on Okinawa and found there was plenty of room in first class. I didn't know of any other class, and it cost the huge amount of $110. They even served filet mignon for dinner—what a treat! We flew to Shreveport and changed planes and then flew on to Alexandria.

STATESIDE LIFE

When the plane arrived at 8:20 AM Sunday morning, I de-planed, and the most beautiful lady in the world was there to meet me. We left the airport for home, and on the way a bug splattered against the windshield. I thought I would be smart and use a phrase I'd heard on Okinawa, "It took a lot of guts to do that."

She countered with "But he doesn't have guts enough to do it again."

I thought, *I've got a smart girl!* She proved that for the next forty-two years.

When we arrived home shortly after 9:00 AM, Mother met us on the porch. After hugging that marvelous lady, she said to me, "You should have told us when you were coming. Then, others from the family could have been here to greet you."

I answered back, "I didn't want anyone else to greet me."

Since I was dressed in my blues (dress uniform), we went right to church. George had me say a few words and then an-nounced I would preach that evening. Geri had bought me a beautiful sport coat with matching trousers, white shirt, and tie, and I wore that to church that night.

A few days later, George came to me and said, "Son, you are not a sport; you are a preacher." So I gave the jacket away and bought a suit.

Three years later I saw his son, George Jr., dressed in a sports coat. I said, "George, look at that!"

"What?" he asked.

"Your son is wearing a sport coat."

"What's wrong with that?"

"Yes, it's wrong for me to wear a sport coat but not your son!"

It was years before I would wear a sport coat. George believed that every preacher should wear a suit every day.

The next weekend Geri and I drove to Monroe, where Brother Tom Fred Tenney was pastoring. We preached for him that weekend and had five people receive the Holy Ghost. Our wedding was planned for Monday evening, June 15, and when we mentioned that to George, he said, "There is a fellowship meeting that night in Anacoco."

So I said we could get married on Tuesday night. I went to the meeting with George, and when Brother Mangun went to the pulpit, he said, "Brother Arless was supposed to get married tonight but postponed his wedding until tomorrow night so he could be here tonight. Since he wanted to be here that badly, I think he should have my time." All the other preachers agreed. So I was the only preacher that night.

I'm sorry that Geri is not here to write about the wedding. The building was full to overflowing, and many were standing. Words cannot describe how beautiful Geri was! Charles was best man, and Lorene was maid of honor. My brothers were groomsmen—Medford, Bill, and Larry, my brother-in-law. George Sr. was the minister, and George Jr. was the singer.

At the reception, Everett Peavy, my nephew, told me that the bride was stolen. I said, "That's all right; I've kissed her good night already." They drove her around the city, through the graveyard, and finally brought her back to the church.

Geri and I cutting the cake

George L. Glass performed the ceremony

Geri and I leaving for our honeymoon

We left around eleven to drive to Lake Charles. I didn't even reserve a hotel, thinking there would be no problem, but found there was not a room available in Lake Charles. So we drove to Jennings and found a room around 3:30 AM. The next day we drove to New Orleans, spent the night there, and then drove on to Pensacola, Florida. Brother Welsh was in revival, so we went that night, stayed one night there, and started back. We went to Baton Rouge Saturday evening, and Sunday morning we went to church with Brother C. G. Weeks. He asked me to preach that night, so we remained and preached. The morning we were there Brother Weeks announced that my brother George had accepted the pastorate of the church. Brother Weeks had been elected as superintendent of the Louisiana District. Monday morning we drove back home. What a honeymoon!

Louisiana camp meeting was beginning the next week. I was still in the air force and was assigned to Carswell AFB, Fort Worth, Texas. Before I left Okinawa, they asked me where I would like to be stationed in the States. I was to give the three choices. None of my choices was in Texas as I had completed basic training in Wichita Falls and didn't want to go back. So they assigned me to Texas. I did my best to stay out of Texas, and when we began our ministry, I asked the Lord please not to let it be in Texas. I called the base and asked them to give me an extension on my leave as I wanted to attend the camp meeting. Also, I was to meet the board to be ordained. George had insisted that I not request a general license but full ordination. The board did not question me at all. All they did was praise me for the work done on Okinawa.

I'll explain how the board was so well informed about Okinawa. I wrote Geri a letter every day, and about once a week I wrote a letter to George. I received a letter every day from Geri—never did I receive a letter from George. I would tell him about those I baptized and the work I was doing. I told him about the classes I was conducting and the opposition, too. I would send him pictures of me baptizing people. I didn't know it, but he was turning over a report to the Foreign Missions Board as well as the editors of the *Pentecostal Herald*. He would then take a letter I had written and write one as if I were writing it to the organization. I knew nothing of this, of course. He mentioned that I was getting opposition from the chaplains. Someone received a *Herald*, clipped a picture of me baptizing an Okinawan and the letter about the opposition I was receiving, and sent it to the wing chaplain of my base on Okinawa. I was called on the carpet for the picture and the letter. I explained to him that I knew nothing about it, but it gave them more ammunition to use against me. George showed the letters to the Louisiana Board, of which he was a member. That was all they wanted to talk about when I went up for ordination.

When Gus returned from Okinawa, he went to see his mom, dad, and sister, Elizabeth, in New Jersey, and after a couple of weeks with them, he came to DeRidder to meet Lorene, whom he had been writing for the past two years. My family fell in love with him and from then on considered him a member of the family. He had to report to McDill AFB in Florida, but he made many trips from there to DeRidder. In only a few weeks, he and Lorene were married. Geri was her matron of honor and I was best man at the wedding. George performed the ceremony.

Before I went overseas, I sold my car to my sister Blanche. When I thought I was coming home in January, I told Geri to order a 1953 Ford Club Coupe. It came to the dealership in January, but I didn't make it home then. It was two-tone blue and beautiful.

After reporting to Carswell AFB, I saw that I was not needed as there was a surplus of men in the chaplain service. I was working only four days a week and asked my first sergeant if it was possible to get a discharge. He laughed at me as I still had fifteen months to go on my enlistment. I told him I was going to write the Pentagon to ask for an early out. Again, they laughed at me. I wrote the letter and explained why I would like to be discharged. I wanted to enter the ministry. I loved the air force and would have made a career of it if it were not for the ministry. I mentioned my two years overseas and the fact that I wasn't needed any longer in the military. The Pentagon notified my wing to discharge me and gave the date as 16 October 1953.

We had three days off, so we went home to DeRidder. The Oldsmobile dealership was across the street from the Gill residence. I walked over, and they had an "eighty-eight" with air conditioning on the floor. Mr. Porter, the dealer, came to me and said, "Let me sell you this car."

"No," I said, "I have a car."

He asked what kind of car I had, and I told him. He said, "I'll give you your money back and give you the air conditioning if you will trade."

We talked for a few minutes, and soon I traded for the four-door car. I knew that evangelizing in a club coupe would be rather small, and the air conditioning would be so nice.

EVANGELIZING

I went back to the base, took a leave in September, and went to the General Conference. At the Conference I went before the Foreign Missions Board and explained the work in Okinawa. They asked me to preach on Foreign Missions day. As a result, they raised thousands of dollars for a work in Okinawa. I began to receive invitations for revivals at the conference. I intended to go to Bible college but was advised against it by my brother, who said the door was open for me. I received my discharge on Friday, October 16, 1953, and drove home that day. The next day I unloaded the car and reloaded it, and we left for a revival the next afternoon with Brother G. A. Mangun in Alexandria.

Our first revival was quite an experience! We were really initiated! We preached over the weekend, and Brother and Sister Mangun left us in order to go to Indianapolis with Brother Nathaniel Urshan. I was to preach Wednesday, Saturday, and Sunday for the next two weeks. The second week, on Saturday evening, I gave the altar call, and one man who had been coming to the altar failed to move. I went back to him to ask why. He said he just didn't want to. I then said to him, "Man, what if you die in this condition?"

He looked at me with wide-open eyes, ran to the altar, and started crying with all his heart. He prayed through before leaving that night. He was in church the next morning.

That afternoon I was called by his daughter to pray for him as he was sick. I said I would come right over, and she said to meet them at the church. The youth service began at 6:00 PM, and as the service began, this man came up for prayer. We gathered around him, anointed him, and with my hand on his head, he died.

I called Brother Mangun and asked him what he wanted me to do. He said, "Preach!"

The ambulance came and removed the body. No one left! I went to the pulpit and started the service. We went through the preliminaries, and I started preaching. There was a heavy anointing on me. I then gave the invitation, and forty-seven people came to the altar!

I said, as I invited the church to come to pray with these, "I don't care if you do have a headache; we need you! Come!" After the altar service, a number received the Holy Ghost. I had about thirty people who were praying with the seekers to come to me and ask for prayer. Each one said, "I have a terrific headache." Brother and Sister Mangun came home the next day. We stayed with them another week and from there went home.

I really didn't want to leave home before the first of the year, so we preached a revival in a small church at Three Pine, Louisiana, and on December 31, we started a revival for George, who was then in Baton Rouge. For the next three years we would close a revival on Sunday and begin the next one on Tuesday. I wanted to preach in as many districts as I could; therefore, we drove many miles between revivals. We would leave after church Sunday night. I would drive until six in the morning and awaken Geri. Then she would drive while I slept a couple of hours. I know it was hard on Geri, but she never complained. She was a perfect evangelist's wife.

We had so many interesting experiences on the evangelistic field that I can't relate them all. We concluded in Baton Rouge and went to West Monroe with Brother Varnado. I was always nervous when the pastor turned the pulpit over to me, we would start with a special chorus. The third or fourth night I rushed to the pulpit with Geri playing the accordion and started the chorus. Geri did not join me and quit playing. I turned and asked her, "Aren't you going to sing?"

She answered, "Which chorus?"

She was playing the chorus we had chosen, and I was singing another. Brother Varnado was off his chair and on his knees laughing, and there were a few laughs from the audience as well. We finally got the right chorus and went on to have a tremendous revival. Missionary Glenn Smith received the Holy Ghost there, as well as many more.

While we were there, Brother Varnado was approved by the Foreign Missions Board to take the work in Jamaica. He asked me if I would consider being pastor of the church in West Monroe. It was a wonderful opportunity, but I felt I was too young and didn't have enough experience to be a pastor. Too, I felt that God wanted me to evangelize.

Geri and I sang one song every night, and she would sing a solo. She was an excellent singer. At that time tape recorders were becoming more common, and someone taped our singing and invited us to their house to listen. When I heard the recording, I never wanted to sing again! I thought, *Those poor people, having to put up with that!* But I continued trying, even though I'm sure I made many more mistakes. It's funny how the mind works; years later, we tend to remember the good things and forget the mistakes we made.

We would begin a revival, and the pastor would have me teach Sunday school, preach morning worship, and preach the evening service. If they had a radio program, they expected me to preach that and any other service they might have during the week. I remember one time we left a revival in DeRidder where they had me preach four times every Sunday, as well as preaching every night of the week. From there we went to De Quincy with Brother Hulon Myre. I said to Geri, "Well, he can't have me preach more than four times on Sunday." The first Sunday was Easter, and he added a special Easter sunrise service. I had five services to preach that day. They kept us busy.

In those days, revivals would run seven nights a week and very rarely under three weeks. When I would make a mistake in word pronunciation, Geri would write it down and correct me after service. I sort of resented it but appreciated it, too. I would look over at her to see her writing and would say to myself, *What have I done now?* I would find out after service. She would never correct me in front of other people, which I appreciated. There was one mistake I made in every revival. I used an illustration of my experience overseas and would say, "He throwed" instead of "He threw." She would correct me every time, but I continued to say the same thing. We were in revival with Brother Nathaniel Urshan, and there must have been a thousand people in the congregation on a Sunday evening. I got on my tiptoes and cried, "He throwed. . . ." Then I looked at Geri and said, "He threw—he threw—he threw." I don't think anyone else caught it, but I never made that mistake again.

I owe so much of my ministry to Geri. I am thankful that she was bold enough to correct me as she did. I shudder to think of how I would be in the pulpit if it were not for her. I learned early that the ministry is a partnership. The wife is a big part of it. I can relate to Solomon's words when he said, "Whoso findeth a wife findeth a good thing, and obtaineth favour of the LORD" (Proverbs 18:22). We stayed in a lot of Sunday school rooms with a rollaway bed. We sometimes ate from plates and silverware that others had discarded. The church did not need anything better; after all, it was only used for five or six weeks a year. We would pull a bench against the door in order to feel safe at night because there were no locks on the doors. We never thought anything of it as every church was struggling financially. We were usually paid one hundred dollars a week, but if we started on Tuesday or Wednesday, we would only get sixty-five dollars or maybe seventy-five dollars. Most of the time, we couldn't start on Sunday because the previous revival closed on Sunday night. We accepted that as just the way it was and never had any extra money. We left Calvary Tabernacle with Brother Urshan, where we were paid 125 dollars a week, and went to a small church in Ohio where they paid us fifty dollars a week. The pastor was in such need that we gave most of it back to him. We preached in West Lake, Louisiana, closed out, and started for home. I said to Geri, "Honey, all our bills are paid and we have twenty-five dollars left." I no sooner had said that when we heard a loud "bang." A blowout! It cost twenty-three dollars for a new tire.

In all, we enjoyed evangelizing even though it must have been hard on Geri, not having any time off. We had to take time off for conferences and camp meetings. That hurt us financially. At the end of the year when we figured our income, it was usually around thirty-five hundred dollars. My brother Bill helped Charles and me so much. He had an insulation business, and when we had a few days off, he would let us work for him. He always seemed to have a house or two that needed to be insulated. He would furnish all the material and give us the full amount of the job.

Charles, Mary Jo, Geri, and I were home one week and decided to go fishing. Molly, Bill's wife, was going with us, and we had the car loaded and ready to go when the phone rang. Charles answered and said to us, "They want us to come to insulate their house! I don't think we will! We're going fishing!"

Mother spoke up, "That's right, boys. When work interferes with fishing, go fishing."

We didn't go fishing. We insulated the house, and the women went fishing. When we finished the insulation job, we returned home, cleaned up, and waited for the girls to come back from the fishing trip. We waited until dark, and Mother was getting worried. We tried to calm her fears, but she insisted we go to look for them. The lake was in Leesville, twenty miles from home. We left in the search, found them in a BBQ place eating, and followed them home.

Bill was home from work and was with Mother when we arrived and everything was all right. Mother said, "These are my daughters, and you can't be too careful with them."

As we discussed the trip later, Bill said, "Well, Mother had a right to worry. They had been gone a long time, it was dark, and anything could have happened. When I am out collecting and don't get home at the proper time, Molly worries about me!" Then he paused and turned to Molly and asked, "You do, don't you?"

In December 1954, we had a six-week revival with Brother Urshan at Calvary Tabernacle. During that time I got sick, and Brother Urshan got me an appointment with his doctor. I went, parked my car on the street, and stayed in the office a little too long. When I went down, my car was gone. I then looked up at a sign on a pole that said, "No parking from 4 to 6 PM." I went to the police station and paid the ten-dollar fine, and they told me where the car had been towed. It was a mile away, the temperature was around zero, and I had to walk. The doctor had told me to go home and not get out of the house for a few days, but I didn't have any choice. So I found the lot, and it was a pitiful place. I went to the office, and they told me it would cost sixteen dollars to get the car out. I didn't have the money so offered to leave my binoculars to hold until I could come back with the money. I wasn't in the best mood at the time, but the man agreed. When I went to church Brother Urshan advanced me sixteen dollars to pay for the storage fee.

We went from there to Logan, Ohio, a small church with about thirty-five members. It was different, to say the least, going from preaching to one thousand on Sunday to thirty-five on Tuesday. That was evangelistic work. We did not "pick" our revivals. We went wherever we were asked, regardless of the size of the church. The Hanbys were members of the Logan church and they were coming to church one Sunday morning when their car hit a patch of ice and slid off the road. The only thing that kept them from a three-hundred-foot drop was a pine sapling about two inches thick, which held their heavy car. When we got there, the family was standing by the car. I can still see the frightened face of Mark, who was about eleven years old at the time. His mother had been driving as Brother Hanby, who was Home Missions Director at the time, was not with them.

I went back to Indianapolis a year later for another revival, and a young lady approached me and asked, "Do you remember when your car was towed away last year?"

I said, "I certainly do!" I thought that maybe Brother Urshan had mentioned this to the whole church.

She then said, "My dad owns that storage lot. He came home that evening and said to us, 'Well, I met your evangelist this evening.' We said, 'How? You've never seen him.' My dad related the story, 'When he walked into my office, I had a strange feeling. Although I had never met him, I knew it was your evangelist.'"

The lady continued, "My dad has been under conviction ever since that night." The Lord doesn't mind making us a little uncomfortable if through that He reaches a soul. I was sorry from that moment that I complained about the ticket.

Our first seven revivals of 1956 were in seven different states. I felt we would not be evangelizing much longer and wanted to get to as many districts as possible. I had no motive in this other than I wanted to meet preachers from all over our fellowship. I also wanted to see as much of the United States as possible. I wanted to see every state in the union. To this day, I have been in every state but five. That bugs me! I have planned trips to these states, but something always happens to keep me from going. I still hope that I will be able to visit them before something happens to me.

PASTORING

A close friend, Virgil Dykes, who was a member of the United Pentecostal church in LaMarque, Texas, approached me and told me they were in need of a pastor. This was a young church, having had three pastors in the four years since its founding. We visited and preached for them and felt there was a good opportunity, so we accepted. They put it to a vote, and we were elected 100 percent. There was a congregation of nineteen with a voting group of nine.

We went there with high expectations and cancelled three years of scheduled revivals to accept the pastorate. I felt that with hard work we could be running two hundred in six months. We worked hard but did not get the results we expected. After five years we had a congregation of 175.

We began our pastorate on November 26, 1956, and had planned to go home for Christmas. We left on December 17, a Sunday night after church, even though I was sick and in much pain driving home. I went to the doctor, and his diagnosis was appendicitis. Dr. Brown operated and told Geri that gangrene had set in and it would be three days before he could say whether I would make it or not. For two days I did great, and my sister Blanche came to see me and said, "I'm glad to see that you are doing so well. The doctor said that if you could make it for three days, you would pull through."

I hadn't heard that, and that night and all the next day I was deathly sick. I thought about what Blanche had said many times during this time. The fourth day I began to feel a little better, but the doctor would not let me go home for Christmas. So I spent the holidays in the hospital. I had no insurance, and even though Doctor Brown did not charge ministers, the hospital bill for the eight days was $217. There I learned how to visit people in the hospital. They are sick! They do not need lengthy visits from anyone. From that time, I keep my visits to three minutes, and on rare occasions, I might stay four minutes.

The doctor had told us that Geri could not have children, but he gave her some medications to try to remedy that. We were blessed the following November 24 by the birth of our first child, Cathy Delayne. It looked as if Mom and Dad Gill had moved in to stay! This was their first grandchild, and Geri was an only child. When they finally went home, I really missed them.

Many of the church members were not too happy about the baby, and it was a while before I found out the reason for this. I was the fourth pastor they had in four years, and it seemed that when the wife had a baby and got able to move around, they resigned. They were afraid that would be the case with us, too. I had to assure them that would not be the case with us. I found out later that when we would leave town for a few days, they would peek in the window to see if our furniture was still there. They soon began to shower affection on Geri, and the church began to grow. It was hard work! A few times it looked as if we would have to leave because of lack of money. The pay was small, and many times we would go to the mailbox and find a letter from a friend with a welcome check in it. Several times we received money from people we did not even know.

One day, Geri and I were sitting at the kitchen table talking about our finances. We needed over a thousand dollars to catch up on our bills. We discussed what to do. When we accepted the church, I foolishly bought a whole house full of furniture on credit. I was not thinking about the low pay and felt that I could have a big church in just a few months. It didn't work out quite like that. I could preach a few revivals, but that would pull me away from Geri and the church. We didn't know what to do!

Then the phone rang. I had purchased an acre of land in De-Ridder while we were evangelizing, and the call was from a man I had known all my life asking if he could buy half of it for fifteen hundred dollars. I answered, "When do you want it?"

He said, "As soon as I can get it."

I told him to have the papers made out, and I would be there the next day. That caught us up on our bills, we paid our tithes, and with the remainder we bought songbooks for the church.

Three years later on November 28, God blessed us with another beautiful girl, Letha Jeane. I had never heard the name Letha before. A short time before, the lieutenant governor of Louisiana, Lether Frazier, had died. In the obituary, it was mentioned that his mother was going to name him Letha after her mother, but since he was a boy, they changed the name to Lether. I liked Letha so much that we gave our second daughter that name. Her middle name was only used when we wanted to reprove her. When Cathy needed rebuking, Geri would say, "Cathy Delayne!" Cathy associated her middle name with trouble, so when she became agitated with her mother, she would say loudly, "Mother Delayne!"

My tenure at LaMarque was probably no different than that of any other pastor who has a home missions church. We were troubled with finances and received very little to live on, but God always provided.

In 1960 we had a hurricane, and the water soaked the sheetrock in the auditorium. I called the insurance company, and they sent an adjuster. He examined the building and could not find any broken windows or roof damage. The rain had blown under the shingles. Because there was no breakage, he would not pay and said to me, "I know the hurricane did this damage, but I can't give you anything. What we can do is leave it alone. When we have another hurricane, if there is breakage, notify us, and we will repair this with the other."

Hurricane Carla came the next year, and it was so bad we had to evacuate the city. When we came back, the church had five shingles broken, and I called the insurance company. The adjuster looked it over and said, "Now, you know that those five broken shingles didn't cause this damage!"

I answered, "I know it and you know it, but you are still going to pay for it." I explained what the other adjuster said to me, and he agreed. We had our walls and ceiling repaired.

About ten of our families had their homes flooded, some with their walls blown down. I went into their homes with them, and we even killed snakes in some of them. Everything they had was destroyed. One couple, Brother and Sister Pierce, lost their home and were left with just the frame standing. Even their second car, which was in the garage, was totally destroyed. What was amazing and unbelievable was that when I entered the front room, a dress lay on the floor with something twisted in it. I picked it up and found a five-dollar roll of dimes and a fifty-cent roll of pennies. The dress had been in the front bedroom closet and the money had been in a chest of drawers in the back bedroom, yet the power of the tornado that hit the house brought them together and laid them on the living room floor. I went to the only restaurant open and ordered a big bag of hamburgers to take to our people, who were working on their homes. It was a sad sight, but all were happy to salvage as much as they did. They also rejoiced that they were all alive.

I went to LaMarque with the intention of staying the rest of my life. Even though I was offered churches in other cities, I couldn't leave. I was offered Fort Worth but turned it down; Mark Hanby accepted it. Then the church in Austin sent someone to talk to me. I turned it down, too, and Kenneth Phillips accepted it.

We had been in LaMarque five years when Brother Steve Galloway resigned from Pasadena. He asked me about coming there, but I brushed it aside. He said to me, "You don't even have to come preach for them; they will accept you if you will consider."

After thinking it over, I finally said that I would preach for them. I prepared my strictest sermon to preach to them that Monday, and as I entered the pulpit I said, "I'm not here to try out for the church. I'm here to see if I want to consider coming."

They wanted me to come back the next night and I did, but Geri would not even come with me. She let me know in no uncertain terms that she didn't like it and did not want to move. I went back and preached and told them that I was not interested.

Then as I was driving away, the Lord spoke to me and said, "Son, you made a mistake. This is your city, and I want you here."

When I arrived home, Geri asked me what I did. I told her that I had turned it down. She then said, "I don't want to hear you complain about this city or this church again!"

"Wait, wait, when have I ever complained about this city or this church?" Then I said, "God has been talking to you!"

"Yes."

"He told you that Pasadena was where we belonged!"

"Yes."

I then told her what God had told me. She asked, "What are you going to do?"

I then called a member of the church board and told him that I would like them to have a vote to see how many of them wanted me to come. The next night, Wednesday, they had a vote, and 100 percent of them wanted me to come. They called me, I accepted, and they had the official election ten days later.

Resigning from the church in LaMarque was one of the hardest things I ever did. After my resignation, I had a birthday, and they gave me a party. They were disappointed in my resignation as we remembered how I had taken the church with twenty in attendance and we had grown to 175. God really blessed there. I was on the road day and night visiting, encouraging, and writing prospects, and I think I won almost all of them myself. No one missed a service without hearing from me, and nobody visited our church without a letter or a visit from me. I would fill the car with gas on Friday evening, and Saturday evening it would be empty. I loved every minute of it. Yes, we had some disappointments and problems, but God brought us through them all. Brother Ralph Sykes was elected as pastor a couple of months later.

We went to General Conference in Kansas City in 1961 and dropped the girls off to stay with Geri's mother in DeRidder. Her father had passed away the year before. We were in a restaurant eating after service the first evening when we got a phone call from Mom Gill. She said that Cathy had a seizure and they rushed her to the hospital. We hurried to our motel, packed our bags, and left immediately. I drove ninety miles an hour all the way and, fortunately, didn't get stopped. When we got to DeRidder, Cathy ran to our arms as if nothing had happened! We went home and took her to our doctor, and after a thorough examination and a lot of questions, he decided that some green pecans she had eaten was the most likely cause of the seizure.

We moved to Pasadena in August 1962. The General Conference was to begin in five weeks after we moved. When it was almost time for us to leave, Geri noticed that Letha's urine was a little clouded. We had planned to drive to DeRidder to drop the girls off with Geri's mom again and then drive to Columbus, Ohio. We decided that because of what happened to Cathy the year before, we should take her to the doctor for a checkup. Since we would be in DeRidder anyway, we decided to take her to Dr. Brown. It turned out that he was too busy to see her, so we saw Dr. Carter, his associate.

Dr. Carter had found a Welm tumor in a five-year-old boy the week before, and because of that he examined all the children who came to him for a tumor. He informed Geri, who called for me to come, and told us that there was a mass in Letha's kidney and he believed it was a Welms tumor.

Dr. Brown came in, pulled me aside, and told me not to worry as Dr. Carter was "hung up" on Welms tumors and thought that every child had one. Welms tumors are very rare and are found in only one in seventy thousand children. At Dr. Carter's insistence, we took her to Lake Charles to Dr. Byrd, who was a specialist. He found the mass but said since we were from Pasadena we should take her back home to see a specialist there.

We took her to a specialist in Pasadena, who put her in Bayshore Hospital for a thorough examination. She had no symptoms of anything being wrong, but once he examined her, he found the tumor. He sent us to M. D. Anderson Hospital, where she was tested again. They wanted to know how we had found the tumor as there were no symptoms of anything wrong. It was the size of a softball. The Welms tumor is called the "silent tumor," and it is not usually detected until it is too late to save the child. The hospital sent us home while they studied on what to do. We had instructions to watch her closely and not to let her fall or throw herself on anything or anyone, as she loved to do. If the tumor should burst, there would be no hope.

That was a torturous week. When we went back to the hospital, they assigned us to Dr. Miller, who was known as the best cancer surgeon in the United States. He worked with three hospitals, one in New York City, one in Chicago, and one in Houston. We went into his office, and he said to us, "There is no hope for your daughter. She will live possibly three months. You will have her to enjoy for that long. There will be no pain and she may hemorrhage, but it is unlikely. She will probably just go to sleep and not wake up."

I asked him about operating, and he said he could but she would not likely survive the surgery. I then said to him, "Doctor, I want you to operate."

He said, "Did you hear what I just told you?"

I said that I did but I still wanted him to operate. He made clear that I would have to take the full responsibility for what happened, and I told him that I understood but still wanted him to perform surgery.

On the day of the surgery, Brothers Killgore and Kershaw came to the hospital to comfort me and saw me smiling, and they thought something was wrong with me. I was talking about comforting the others because I had heard from God. He told me to have them operate, and she would be all right! When they brought her out of surgery, she opened her eyes and said, "Daddy, I'm all right now!" That brought tears to all our eyes!

The next day seven doctors came into her room expecting her to be gone. She was gone all right; we were rolling her up and down the hall.

Dr. Miller came in to check on her, and I saw the length of the incision and said to him, "That's a mighty long incision."

He answered, "I had a mighty big thing to get out of her body."

The nurses told me that during the operation he handled the tumor very carefully. They had learned that the Welms tumor doesn't have roots but shoots seeds if it is punctured. Other doctors would make a small incision and force the tumor out and then send the patient to M. D. Anderson. In just a few weeks, the tumor would be back and the child would die. Out of a thousand children they had at M. D. Anderson with this tumor, only five survived. Letha was one of the five. They later took pictures of her for the world conference on cancer research to show the most amazing recovery they had seen.

Since the tumor was encased in a kidney they felt that they had gotten all of it, but just to be on the safe side they wanted to give her chemotherapy and radiation treatment. Both were new, in the experimental stage, and could stunt her growth, but we accepted the treatment. We took her back for checkups once a week, then every two weeks, then once a month, then once every three months, then once a year. Every time we went back after the examination, I would look over the doctor's shoulder to see what he would write on her chart, and it was always the same. "This is the most amazing recovery I have ever seen."

When Letha married and had a baby, the doctors could not believe it! People from all over the world had prayed for her. The cards, letters, and phone calls were unbelievable! To God be the glory!

PASADENA

Brother Steve Galloway, a former marine of WWII and a hero to me, started the church in Pasadena and then after nine years felt he should move to Colorado. He approached me and asked me if I would accept the church. As I stated earlier, we had to give it some thought and prayer but finally accepted. He surrendered a wonderful church to me. They received us with open arms and fully supported me.

A month after we moved to Pasadena, a saint from another church called, and my mother-in-law answered. The caller said, "I was raised with Brother Glass in DeRidder. My family attends Life Tabernacle, and we have decided to leave and come over to Pasadena."

My mother-in-law said, "That wouldn't be a good idea. You have been there for a number of years and are settled in a good church. You really need to stay where you are." She took her advice.

Since then we have rarely had someone from another church in the area move to be with us. We are here to win the lost, not to pull people from other churches. At the end of the day, what have you done if you have a thousand in attendance and they came from other churches?

God blessed us with growth. When I look back on how great He has blessed, I can pass from the scene contented. We have people all over the world who have come from this church, a number of preachers have gone out from this church, and there are missionaries—foreign and home—who are doing a great work for God. We have started eleven churches over the United States, and most of them are thriving today. We can count over twenty churches in our area that have people who prayed through in this church, and we have seen many miraculous healings, deliverances, and many baptized in the wonderful name of Jesus and filled with the Holy Ghost. Years ago, our mayor and his wife began attending. He quit but she continued. She asked him one day to explain Acts 2:38 to her. His answer was, "It simply means that if will you repent and be baptized in Jesus' name, you will receive the baptism of the Holy Ghost." She came to church the next week and was filled with the Holy Ghost before she could reach the altar. When his term was over, they moved from Pasadena. Since then we have had three mayors who declared publicly that the United Pentecostal Church was the rock of Pasadena. We have seen "Pentecost" reenacted over and over and over again.

After we had been in Pasadena only a year, we were forced to buy more property. We started with just one lot where the church building sat and now have eleven acres, counting the Methodist church property next door. We've had five building programs because of our growth, and there was never a time when we were not paying a building note. The property is worth approximately six million dollars.

When we came to Pasadena, Brother V. A. Guidroz was district superintendent, and he was one of my mentors and became like a father to me. It was in his heart to have a Bible college in Texas. He called for a special district conference to be held in Bryan, Texas to discuss the proposal. Brother Murray Burr wrote the resolution, Brother Guidroz called for it, and Brother

Kilgore and I brought it to the floor for a vote, where it passed by 100 percent. The three of us were appointed to a committee, along with Marvin Hicks, J. T. Pugh, Fred Foster, Hulon Myre, and Titus McDonald to start the Bible college. After many meetings, Houston was chosen as the site. Brother Kilgore found an apartment we could purchase, and I found the financing. We wanted to build new, but the cost was so prohibitive, we felt we could not afford it. Fred Foster was chosen as the first president, and the committee became the Board of Directors. We were wise in choosing Brother Foster as he made a tremendous leader. Brother Foster felt it wise to choose as many pastors as he could to the faculty. I will try to remember each one: James Kilgore, Murray Burr, J. T. Pugh, L. L. Stevens, Orlin Ray Fauss, O. W. Williams, Fred Olson, Clark Lott, C. L. Dees, and me.

T. F. Tenney and I receiving honorary doctorates
from Apostolic Bible Institute

During Brother Foster's tenure we had a high of 450 students, and it was exciting to be on the campus. Classes began on January 4, 1964. I taught there for fourteen years and was teaching there when I was appointed superintendent of education for the UPCI. Because of this, I could no longer be associated with any particular college. I have never been to college, so it was a tremendous honor to teach at Texas Bible College. I was approved by the Texas Board of Education, and through my teaching of many subjects I earned a Bachelor of Theology degree in 1975. I was also awarded an honorary doctorate degree in Pentecostal studies by Apostolic Bible Institute. World Academy of Letters awarded me a master's diploma. I gave my lesson outlines on "The Life of Christ" to the Foreign Missions Division of the UPCI, and they translated them into different languages and have been using them in over one hundred Bible colleges outside the United States for thirty years. I have a copy of my outlines in Greek. Dorsey Burk from Global Missions took my outlines, put them in book form, and recently published the book. It is offered by Pentecostal Publishing House.

On April 20, 1966, Darryl Richey Glass was born. What a joy! The day he was born, a number of our church members were at the hospital, and when I walked out of the delivery room, I wasn't smiling. They looked at me, and someone said disappointedly, "It's a girl!" I then beamed and said, "No, it's a boy!" They all smiled and rejoiced with me. I called Charles and told him that I now had a son whose name is Darryl, after Iva Glass Augenstein's son who was killed in a plane crash. He then told me that his dog had just had a litter of puppies, and he named every one of them Arless. He was able to be with us when we brought Geri and Rich home from the hospital.

I am so proud of my son. He has become one of the best preachers I have ever heard and also one of the best singers around. God jumped over a generation to give him a beautiful voice for music.

Although I had carried a heavy load as pastor, teacher at the Bible college, and other duties, it was worth it. I sometimes wonder how big our church would be if I could have devoted all my time to being a pastor, even though I never neglected the church. I shall list at the end of this book the many offices I have held throughout my years in the ministry.

In 1975 Geri and I went with Brother and Sister Chambers to the Philippines for a conference and preaching tour. It was a strange experience to look out the window and see soldiers walking in the churchyard, carrying sub-machine guns. After we came home, our church furnished the money to buy a large boat that they desperately needed in the Philippines.

In 1976, I was invited to visit Ghana by our missionaries Robert and Sissy Rodenbush. I took a young man from our church, Louis Johnson, with me. We went to teach in their Bible college on the subject of leadership, a subject I happened to be teaching at Texas Bible College. I didn't know what to expect in the way of food and remembered the food when we visited the Philippines the year before. The fruit was the only thing I really enjoyed. I had my camera case that had some extra room, so I bought candy bars—Snickers, Mars, Milky Way, and Hershey bars—as many as my case would hold. I thought that I would at least enjoy that. I'm afraid I thought I could live on the candy bars.

Robert Rodenbush and Louis Johnson,
who would become a missionary in Uganda

A group of ministers I taught in a class in Ghana

We arrived in Ghana after twenty-three hours on a 707 that was so fully loaded that the seats would not recline. The Rodenbushes met us at the airport and took us to their home. I found that their son, Rob, had not seen a candy bar in a long time, so I took my camera out of the case, turned the case over on the table, and gave him my hoard of candy. I know he enjoyed it! When Brother Tom O'Daniel said, "I wish you could have brought some milk," I felt sorry that I didn't know, or I would have tried. I remembered how those fresh eggs tasted to me after being without them for eighteen months. I found that the things we take for granted here mean so much to our missionaries. We taught for two weeks in their college and then preached at a few places. It was really enjoyable, and I can say that Brother and Sister Rodenbush cannot be beaten as Christians and hosts. I didn't suffer one bit over the food as Sister Rodenbush is a wonderful cook, and it was just like home. The preachers of Ghana are some of the finest brethren in the world, and they loved the Rodenbushes. Those missionaries were sorely missed when they were called back to the States. We went from there to Kenya with the Ikerds, who had a wonderful work there. As a result of our trip, Louis and Martha Johnson are now missionaries to Uganda, Africa.

After my appointment as superintendent of education in 1977, I was appointed military endorsing agent for the UPCI. I questioned Brother Chambers, our general superintendent at the time, about it. He informed me that the government required every church denomination to have one. Brother Cleveland Becton, as general secretary, was designated as such, but they wanted me to have the office. I told him that if I had that office, I wanted to work on getting UPCI chaplains in the military. After working in the chaplaincy during the Korean War, I saw the blessings and the need for our church to have a military ministry. He gave me the green light to do what I wanted, but as I began looking into it, I found that we had a serious problem. Not one of our Bible colleges was accredited. The reason was that the American Association of Bible Colleges, the accrediting agency, would not accept us because we could not sign their doctrinal statement. It states that there are three persons in the Godhead; namely Father, Son, and Holy Ghost. Unless we ascribed to that, we could not be endorsed. The president of the association told me personally that we would never be accredited through their agency unless we changed our doctrine. There was no way we could accept that as we believe there is one person in the Godhead. We believe that God is Father in divinity, Son in humanity, and Holy Ghost in experience. His name is Jesus! First Timothy 3:16, "God was manifest in the flesh." So they turned us down for accreditation.

I asked Brother Nathaniel Urshan, who had become our superintendent, if I could press a lawsuit against them. He did not think that was a good idea so refused me permission to proceed with the suit. The military then turned us down. As a result, we threatened a discrimination lawsuit and the army said, "Don't do that! We can work something out." They decided if our candidates could take their transcripts to an accredited seminary and say they had the equivalence of an accredited degree, they would accept us. Brother Gary Truman submitted, and they accepted him as the first chaplain of the United Pentecostal Church International. He made such a favorable impact that they contacted me and asked, "Do you have any more like Gary Truman? We will accept all you can give us." That began a successful ministry for the UPCI. At present we have thirty chaplains in all branches of the military, a number in seminary preparing for the chaplaincy, and eight retired chaplains. I did this work without a salary, and to this date I am still the endorsing agent.

In study perhaps thirty years ago I read that God commanded the Jewish people, when they woke up in the morning, to say as their first words, "Hear, O Israel: The LORD our God is one LORD." After reading that, I thought if it pleased the Lord for them to do so, I am sure it would please the Lord for us to do so as well. You can say it is Old Testament, but it is the foundation of the Bible and of our church. Because of that, I started quoting the verse each morning as I awakened. I guess I go just a little bit further: I say "Hear, O Arless: The Lord thy God is one Lord, and His name is Jesus." Then I continue, "And thou shalt love the Lord thy God with all thine heart, with all thy soul, with all thy might, and with all thy strength. And thou shalt love thy neighbor as thyself." I have been quoting that for about thirty years, every morning. I love it! I love to meet the day with that passage and that truth.

About four years ago, my grandson, Garrett, volunteered for the Marines. After a few weeks' training he was sent to Afghanistan. The Lord strongly impressed me to have his family read Psalm 91 each evening before retiring, reading it aloud. That is considered the "soldier's psalm." I started reading it each day, and I haven't missed an evening reading it aloud. I cannot think of retiring without reading aloud that psalm. It is from God and contains many promises for us. I refuse to memorize it; I want to read it.

A pilot explains to me the workings
of a Black Hawk helicopter

Chaplain Pentecost

There are a group of men we have in the ministry,
Who dedicate their lives to serve wherever it may be.
Some choose evangelism, some on the mission field,
Others the work of pastor; and do so with great zeal.

Still others find God's call to be in the military chaplaincy,
Ministering to those in uniform and serve our great country.
The United States of America, the greatest of the great!
But without God within her midst, what an awful fate!

These men, we call Chaplain Pentecost, serve our country well;
The blessings they are to all our troops, time alone will tell.
Daily their lives are "on the line" on the battlefields abroad;
Even at home the risks are there, in the service of their God!

We say a great big "thank you," yet that seems so small.
We see you in your uniform, standing so straight and tall.
A patriot, a friend, a counselor; a servant of the Lord,
Desiring to be used of God, and move with one accord.

The church is pleased as you serve in the uniform of your choice;
The men and women you have won cause us to rejoice!
Continue on, O men of God, and know the church can see
The work is great; rewards are high, for all eternity!

Your endorsing agent, Arless Glass

Me, Chief of Chaplains Brigadier General Carver, and
Chaplain Lieutenant Colonel Raymond Robinson as he received
an award as chaplain of the year

Daniel Batchelor; me; the US Chief of Naval Chaplains; and
Gary Truman, the first UPCI chaplain

Me, Chief of Chaplains Brigadier General Baldwin, and Daniel Batchelor

Our first nine chaplains with General Superintendent Nathaniel Urshan, General Secretary Cleveland Becton, and me

Me and Joan in front of the car assigned to us while in Korea in 2008

THROUGH THE YEARS

In 1979, Geri noticed a lump in one of her breasts. She went immediately to the doctor, and he assured her it was nothing to worry about, just a calcium deposit. We did worry, though. She went to another doctor and a third doctor, and they all said the same thing. She went back every six months until 1982, and they gave us the same report each time.

As we were preparing to go overseas to visit some chaplains, she checked again with the doctor, and he said, "To relieve your concerns, when you come back from the trip we'll make you an appointment with a cancer specialist. He will assure you that you have nothing to worry about."

When we returned, she went to the specialist. He took one look and said, "You have cancer, and you have waited too late for treatment!" Our world came crashing in upon us!

He scheduled surgery, and when it was over, the doctor came out of the operating room with a startled look on his face and said to me, "I got it! I got it! There are no roots at all. She's going to be all right!" The roots that he had seen on the x-rays were gone! You can imagine the rejoicing that went on in that waiting room. She took radiation and chemotherapy and was pronounced free of cancer. She stayed clear for nine years, and during that time, her case was used by the doctors to testify to others about breast cancer. Then she began to have pain in her back, between her shoulders. Going to her oncologist, she discovered that the cancer had come back and was in her backbone. She began chemotherapy and radiation. This time each treatment made her deathly sick for a week. After a period of time she could no longer lie on the bed and had to spend her nights sleeping in a recliner. The people of the church were so wonderful, and someone was with her throughout the day, every day. I took her in a wheelchair with me when I could. I had a special device installed in the room that she could pull up with and get in her wheelchair.

In July 1994, we went to the summer seminar I had instituted upon my appointment as superintendent of education. It was a time for all the leaders of our Bible colleges to get together, share notes, and learn from each other. We held it in various places, and this year it was in Toronto, Canada. Our room was on the third floor of the hotel, across from the elevator. The third night, at 2:00 AM the fire alarm sounded. It was right outside our door, yet we didn't hear it. Gus and Lorene were in the room next door, and they heard it and evacuated to the ground floor. It was loud enough to raise the dead, yet we didn't hear a thing. God performed a miracle for us that night. There would have been no way I could have gotten her downstairs without the elevator—which they would not allow once the fire alarm sounded. To try would have inflicted such intense pain she couldn't have stood it! As it turned out, the fire was a small one in the kitchen and was soon extinguished with very little damage.

A group of ladies had gotten together and agreed to call Geri every day. They were Lorene Gustafson, Sissy Rodenbush, Jerry Ann Guidroz, Sue Jackson, Shirley Welch, and Joyce Jones. Each of them called faithfully on her designated day until my wife passed away. They were a great comfort and blessing to her. At her death they were honorary pallbearers.

She eventually got so low that we had to take her to the hospital on February 2, 1995. She suffered almost unbearable pain, and they had to put an air mattress on the bed so she could lay for the first time in over a year. She said to me, "Honey we'll have to get one of these; I can lie down."

She had been in the hospital for two weeks when she called for Cathy, Letha, Rich, and me to come to her bedside. She asked each of us a question. "Will you give me up? Will you allow God to take me?"

Not one of us wanted to say yes, but because of her intense suffering we knew we could not hold her here any longer. So we said, "Yes."

She smiled and told us how much she loved us, and I quoted the poem, "Should You Go First." When I finished, we were all in tears.

Shortly, we walked out of the room, and I told the children, "I asked the Lord last August when He was going to do something for Geri. I got the answer, 'Come spring!' So we have another month to go."

Then Letha said to me, "But, Dad, spring comes early this year!"

I will admit that I told the Lord, "You don't have to wait until spring. She is suffering so much that I am willing for You to take her now if You are not going to heal her." The hospital had given us an extra room for us to have prayer meetings. Someone was there continually praying.

Another miracle happened there. She wanted to see Lorene so badly before she died, but she never told me this. If I had known how close to death she was, I would have gotten Lorene to the hospital anyway.

During February 21, Cathy House was entering the hospital to see Geri when she saw Gus and Lorene at the elevator on the ground floor. She ran toward the elevator to tell them where Geri's room was, but the doors closed before she could get there.

The lady who was in Geri's room saw the door open, but nobody came in. In a few minutes the door opened and closed again, but again she saw no one. A few minutes later, Cathy came in and asked, "Where are Brother and Sister Gustafson?"

The lady answered, "They haven't been here."

Cathy said, "I saw them enter the elevator and come to this floor. I'll go and look around this floor to see if I can find them." They couldn't be found.

On the evening of the same day, Geri's last day on earth, an administrator of the hospital approached the group praying in the special room and told them that the hospital had to have the room. However, the lobby could be used as they locked the doors at 10:00 PM; thus, nobody would bother them. They were there at midnight when they saw the two front doors open and close, then the next two open and close, then the elevator doors open and close. They saw no one! The numbers on the elevator indicated that it stopped at the second floor. A few minutes later the same thing happened in reverse. It was 12:05 AM. A prophecy had been given a couple of days earlier that said the angels were waiting outside to take Geri home.

The hospital staff and the doctor insisted we leave the hospital at 10:00 PM for a few hours. We wanted to stay and go to the prayer room, but they answered, "She will know that you are here! Leave, and give her time to pass. She won't pass until you leave!"

Reluctantly, we went home. My brother Charles, Wayne McClain, and Ronny Guidroz stayed at the hospital. Then at ten minutes after twelve, they called us to come—she had passed.

We rushed to the hospital to her room, had prayer, and shed more tears as we continued talking to her. Who knows when the spirit left the room? After two hours they came for her body; we followed her as far as we could go and then went outside, looked up, and noticed the trees were budding. Spring had come! It is still heartbreaking today as I write this.

There were over two thousand at her funeral in Pasadena. We buried her in DeRidder in the family plot, and there were more than five hundred at the cemetery for her burial. The amazing fact is that God only took His part of Geri, but He left me with my part—the wonderful memories of so many years together.

It seemed that her death took all the joy out of living! We were married forty-one years and eight months. Geri was a remarkable woman! I shudder to think what I would have been without her. She was brilliant! In her last months, she directed the ladies' work from her recliner through Sister Audrey Laborde. All the ladies were so faithful to her and the work of the church. I'm glad the church decided to keep me after she was gone. No one knows the loneliness unless they have experienced it. You feel as if you are a "fifth wheel" and don't fit anywhere. Friends are there to encourage you in every way they can, and you appreciate them. You are thankful for them. You don't refuse to be comforted, but the hurt is so deep that nothing said or done really affects you. You almost feel like digging a big hole, crawling into it, and pulling it in with you!

Our general superintendent, Nathaniel Urshan, sent his administrative assistant, Tom Jackson, with orders to stay with me until I felt I could be alone. Brother Jackson is like my own brother. I was so thankful for his coming. Also, Gus came and stayed with me. They were so valuable to me.

I really didn't think I could ever consider marrying again. A few months after Geri's death, I was praying when out of the clear blue God spoke to me and said, "I have prepared JoAnn Cannon for you."

I said, "No! I don't want someone that young."(I thought she was about forty-nine years old at the time). I was acquainted with her as the Ladies' president of the Louisiana District but knew nothing about her and had never thought about her. I was not ready for that move.

About a year later, I attended a General Board meeting in Saint Louis. Certain ones, namely the Tenneys, Jacksons, Rodenbushs, and Bectons, invited me to dinner. I went with the Jacksons, and when we were seated, there was an empty chair next to me. In a minute JoAnn walked in and said to me, "Why, Brother Glass, have you saved this chair for me?"

I was somewhat surprised but said, "Why, yes," and got up and held the chair for her.

She whispered to me, "They have arranged this, so let's put on a show." So we laughed and talked to each other, ordered a dessert, and shared it. Their jaws dropped at the table when they saw our friendliness. Then when we started to leave, she and I talked together at the door for a few minutes while they were getting ready to leave. I think they were congratulating themselves for having a successful dinner.

The next month was a "Because of the Times" conference, so I called her and asked her to go with me. She refused but said, "I plan to go, and if there is a seat next to you, I will sit with you." That started the speculation!

After the service we were going to the Manguns' house along with many others, so she went with me. As we walked across the parking lot to my car, she took my hand and held it until we got to the car. She said later that it was an unconscious act. I knew then that God had spoken to her also.

We were at General Conference in San Antonio having our chaplains' banquet when she was asked to say a word. She mentioned how much she enjoyed the banquet and she hoped she would be invited back. Someone said, "What about that, Brother Glass?"

Then I spoke up and through the microphone said, "JoAnn, will you marry me?" That brought the house down.

"What about it?" they shouted. I thought for a moment that she was going to say no.

She said, "Brother Glass, if you will go ahead and dismiss, I guess I will."

We purchased the marriage license the first part of December, and all our children had gathered for Christmas on the twenty-first. The children said, "We're all here; why don't you two get married right now?"

After some talking, she in her regular dress and me in my blue jeans stood before Rich, and in a very short ceremony, he married us. When our gathering was over, she went with her kids to their hotel to spend the night, and the next morning they were in church. Bill Davis was preaching for us, and I said, "We are so glad to have JoAnn and her family with us today."

Bill spoke up and asked, "What is her last name?"

"Glass," I answered. Then the whole church shouted.

Her home church in Coushatta, Louisiana, wanted to give us a proper wedding, so we went there two weeks later. They had a big wedding for us with a reception and all the trimmings.

At the next General Board meeting in January, Brother Urshan dismissed the board for a wedding reception in our honor. Brother and Sister Urshan were such tremendous friends and treated us royally. Everyone was so nice and wanted to have pictures taken with us at the reception.

JoAnn and me with the Urshans

JoAnn was just an extension of Geri. She was wonderful and so beautiful and talented. Never a cross word, never a raised voice, always a smile. What a lady! I know I didn't deserve her but was so very thankful for her! She won the hearts of our church family right away.

Five years later we went to Europe to visit our chaplains and had a wonderful time. One night toward the end of our stay, I heard a loud bump on the floor. I jumped up, and JoAnn had fallen and hit her head. She was unconscious and appeared to be dead. I prayed for her for quite a while, and she finally woke up. She told one of her friends later that she died in that room, although she never told me that. She was under a doctor's care before we left, and she immediately reported to him on our return. I do not know what she told him about that experience, if she did. He said that she would have withdrawals from a certain medicine she was taking and might think it was a heart attack but not to worry as she would be over it in just a short while.

Becky came to be with us and to talk to the doctor around the twentieth of October. The doctor assured both of us that

JoAnn was fine and for us not to worry. Becky went home that same day.

On October 25, 2002, we went to the Methodist hospital, where they gave her an iodine injection as part of some tests. We left there and went to lunch and from there went home. She was feeling well and went to Wal-Mart to walk. She came home, and we were sitting in the den talking about what the doctor had said. She was laughing and saying that we don't have to worry about having cancer, when she suddenly said, "Something's happening!"

I rushed to her and started praying. The power of God came down so strongly, I don't believe I have ever been so close to Heaven as at that moment! I started to speak in a language that I had never spoken in! Brother Tenney called this "the tongue of angels."

I realized she was gone and called 911, then called my children. They met us at the ER, and we were in the room as they worked to revive her but finally said, "It's no use, she's gone." I called her doctor, and he seemed totally shocked!

Rich called Becky and Tom Jackson, and they both came the next morning. Tom had stayed with me when Geri died and now was with me with JoAnn. Before the funeral he and I were at my home sitting at the dining table when we heard a loud crash. We couldn't figure out what it was. We began to look around and found where JoAnn had a crystal cake plate over one-half-inch thick with a cup and saucer in it. It had broken in the middle, a clean break, without hurting the cup and saucer. Neither one of us could understand why it broke! It looked like it had been broken with a tool because it was such a clean break. I told that to my children, and Rich said, "JoAnn just met Mother."

I had trouble getting an autopsy report from the hospital or doctor. Finally, I succeeded, thinking something was wrong they didn't want me to know. I called my niece, Charla Aldous, an attorney, and asked her if I could send it to her. She took it to Baylor College of Medicine, and the president and his board studied it. They informed me that since she had to die, this was the best way for her to go. Her entire cardiovascular system was diseased, and she could have started hemorrhaging in any part of her body at any time.

At the funeral someone started speaking in tongues; another interpreted and said, "I loaned her to you at a time of need, and now I have called her home."

I can say, "Thank God for the loan!" She was a tremendous blessing to me and my family as well as the church family for the nearly six years I had her. I wanted to spend the rest of my life with her, but that was not God's plan. Her daughter and son-in-law, Becky and Geron Davis, are still my children. I love them and Neiman and Gerica as my very own.

I thank God for friends! Brother Nathaniel Urshan sent Tom Jackson to Pasadena and told him to stay with me as long as I needed him. Robert Rodenbush also came to be with me. Gus came and stayed with me as well. Tom and Gus are just like blood brothers. Words cannot express how much I appreciate them, along with Brother Rodenbush.

Me and JoAnn with Tom and Sue Jackson

When I married JoAnn Cannon, someone told her that I was "rich as cream." She found out before we were married that was not true. Yet I am rich, rich in the love of God, His blessings, His mercies, His grace. I would not trade the riches that I have for anything in the world. If riches come by giving, I am rich! I cut my salary sixteen times during my ministry; never did I cut it when I could afford to do so. The church needed it. We have been continually in a building program, thus constantly in need of finances. I assure you that most preachers don't get rich pastoring a church. They could, if they took everything offered to them, but we are here to build the kingdom of God, not to build our own little kingdom. I have had people seek to make me rich, but I always refused. I have the philosophy that, as Paul said, "They which preach the gospel should live of the gospel" (I Corinthians 9:14).

Every preacher is aware that he must be first in everything. When the church is in need, he is the first to know and respond. At all special meetings—camp meetings, conferences, and rallies—the pastor is asked to contribute the most. In the local church when a need is realized, he acts first. If he can take care of the need personally, he will. When we planned our new church building, we counted the cost as best we could. Our plans were drawn, and a bid was received that met our estimate of 750,000 dollars. We studied our finances to see if we could make the seven-thousand-dollar monthly note and decided that it would be close but we could do it.

We started our new building in November 1978. The first load of steel came, and we paid for it. Then inflation took off! The second load of steel came, and it had doubled in price in two weeks. From there prices began to go out of sight. We would receive a bid from a contractor, and it would only be good for two or three weeks. There was no way we could stop the building program because we had torn down our auditorium to build on that site. We had to continue. We went back to the bank to increase our loan. The original loan interest rate was 7 percent, and they now wanted 14 percent. The principal was increased to one million dollars. I cut my salary, sold my car, bought a used one, and made more adjustments. When we had the building finished enough to move in, we had gone over our increase by one hundred thousand dollars.

I had never had to go to a relative to ask for anything, but now I felt that I must. I wrote a letter to my cousin, Iva Augenstein, asking her for a loan of one hundred thousand dollars. I made sure she knew that if she could not do it that it would not hinder our friendship in any way. I was jogging every night from eleven to twelve on the school track near my home, and one night Geri came to get me and said that Iva's brother, Gerald, had called. I rushed home to call back, and he said, "Iva received your letter and wants you to come over; she will have the money waiting for you." I hung up and shouted, then went back to the track to finish my run. I believe that I floated around that track to complete my four miles. We were in the church, but it was not finished. In addition, our note was not seven thousand dollars per month but now $11,600. We had not planned for that much and could never pay it on time.

This went on for two years until one morning at 4:30 I went to the church and had a prayer meeting. I began walking around the auditorium and rebuking the devil! I said, "Satan, get your hands out of our finances." I did that for thirty minutes. From that time, we were able to meet our note on time. We never had money left over, but we were able to pay our bills. The people wanted to finish the building on the inside. I cashed in all my insurance policies, except one. I felt that I should keep one so the church could be covered partially should anything happen to me. I also cashed in my retirement policies. I put all the money in the church building program, and we finished the building.

In 2008 Hurricane Ike destroyed our church, the insurance would not pay us enough to complete the needed repairs, and we lost some people during the two and one-half years we were in a rented building. Because of this the church was in need again. I canceled the insurance policy that I had kept, took the money, and gave it to the church. What did I need it for? A lady had given me a new Avalanche in 2002, and it should last me the rest of my life. The Lord is taking care of all my other needs.

On my sixtieth birthday, I was praying and said, "Lord, I am sixty years old today. In five years I will be retirement age, and I do not have one penny saved for it. What am I going to do?"

Then the Lord spoke to me strong and clear, saying, "Don't worry about that! I am going to take care of you!"

Today, I am eighty-two years old and can say, "He is faithful!" My cousin notified me that she was canceling the loan she had given me, and I gave the church one hundred thousand dollars.

In 1994, I went to Canada to dedicate a refurbished Bible college. I stayed over the weekend and was asked to preach at a beautiful country church. In front of the church was the best bass lake in the region. A member mentioned that he had recently seen a fourteen-point buck on his property. The pastor resigned that morning. I preached that Sunday evening also, and before I left, I was approached and asked if I would consider pastoring them. I said, "Your church is beautiful and you have many things I admire here, but I am afraid that I can't accept. I would love to, but I know I can't."

About three months later I was praying, and the Lord spoke to me, "Son, I answered your prayer!"

I said, "Thanks, Lord. Which prayer are You talking about?"

He replied, "Years ago you asked that when you turned sixty-five I would give you a nice country church near a good fishing lake and good hunting. I offered it to you!" I had turned sixty-five a month before the trip to Canada.

Another lesson the Lord taught me: I felt the Lord was through with me in Pasadena. I wanted to leave and go to Austin. I wrestled with that for about three months. One Sunday the secretary of the church in Austin came to be with us. After service, he approached me and said that they wanted me to take the church in Austin. Everything in me wanted to say, "Yes!" I answered, "No, I don't think I can!"

They asked me if I would think about it for a week. I said, "I will, but I'm sure I will not accept it. Don't let me keep you from finding someone else."

That afternoon, I went to my knees and said, "God, I don't know what is wrong with me. Everything in me says You are through with me here, but I am not moving one inch until You tell me what is going on!"

He answered me in a strange way. He said, "Son, how long were you in LaMarque?"

I was startled by that and, after thinking a few minutes, said, "Five years and nine months."

He then said, "How long have you been here?"

I counted again and said, "Five years and six months."

He then said, "There is your answer." He was informing me that my subconscious mind was trying to take over, convincing me that it was God. When I recognized that the burden for Pasadena was back, I understood. I am now in my fiftieth year here and could have missed it so easily. Kenneth Phillips was then called to Austin, and he accepted.

I have come to understand why preachers move so often. I knew some who stayed for three years and moved, then stayed in the next church for three years. Others would not stay over seven years. I now believe that when God calls you to a place, it is for life. I went to LaMarque because I wanted to settle down, they needed a pastor, and I felt I could help them. But when I came to Pasadena, the Lord spoke to me very plainly and told me He wanted me here—that this is my city. I can't leave until He tells me I can.

I have been afraid to seek riches elsewhere because once I start a project, I want to devote all my time to that. This might cause me to neglect the work of God.

The United Pentecostal Church International has been good to me! I owe them my life! I have been in church all my life, at first as a sinner, then at eighteen receiving the Holy Ghost. I have been highly privileged to know every leader of this organization. Brother Howard Goss was the first general superintendent after the UPC was formed in 1945. I met him, became friends with him, and thought he was one of the greatest. You should have heard him pray! Chills would run up your spine just to listen.

When Brother Goss retired, Brother A. T. Morgan was elected. He was a personal friend from my hometown of DeRidder. He would drive to Pasadena from DeRidder to visit us. Geri would cook a meal, and we would have a wonderful time talking. He and Brother Tom Tenney came one day, and Geri fixed a deer roast. I didn't tell them what it was, and they kept coming back for more.

When Brother Morgan died in 1967, Brother Stanley Chambers was elected, and he was also a personal friend of mine. He came to Pasadena to ask me if I would serve at headquarters. He wanted me to serve in Home Missions, but I had to refuse. I told him I would be glad to serve in any position as long as I could remain at the Pasadena church. Three weeks later I received a letter that I was appointed as superintendent of education.

When Brother Chambers retired, Brother Nathaniel Urshan was elected. When I needed help, he was right there for me. I handled a case in 1968-70 that caused me to be very unpopular, and few stood with me. Brother Urshan declared himself for me all the way through. Thankfully, we came out winners in the case. He helped me in my position in Education by attending many of our special seminars and meetings.

Another personal friend since the 1950s, Brother Kenneth Haney, was elected when Brother Urshan retired, and now Brother David Bernard is the superintendent of the UPCI. He and I have been friends for many years. When I retired from Education, I was happy the General Board to approved Daniel Batchelor to take my place. The newly appointed superintendent then turned to me and said, "Brother Glass, you may be retiring from your position but not from the Board of Education. You will remain there and remain as endorsing agent as long as you are able."

Many are not aware of my position as superintendent of education and as military endorsing agent. I have had numbers approach me, asking to recommend them for positions upon my retirement. When they are told of the salary involved, they change their minds. Those are jobs where the only pay is expenses. There is no fundraising and thus no money coming in. When I accepted the position, I was told that my expenses would be paid, and they were. But there was no expense for salary. The Pentecostals of Pasadena took care of my needs as their pastor and would take care of many of the needs of the division of education. It is a work of love. I received no offerings as I was continually working with colleges that thought we were being paid by headquarters and were not obligated to give an offering. Complain about it? Certainly not! That is the work of God! God always takes care of His people. Since we had no office at headquarters, people considered us part-time. Of course we did a full-time job with no pay and no part-time salary. Reverend Batchelor, knowing this, was more than willing to assume the responsibilities of this office. He is doing a superb job and definitely has a burden for it. I am thrilled over the burden God has given him for our chaplains. He is like a son to me. He and his wife Nilah, are doing a tremendous job in Education, and I know they will do well in the Chaplaincy. I thank God for them.

The Board of the Division of Education

I really planned never to marry again. It does get mighty lonely living alone. I've eaten so many hot dogs that I could not begin to number them. I would buy a package of buns and a package of wieners and each day have one until I ran out, then buy more. I guess I really saved on my grocery bill. I really hated to eat out by myself. I could have gone with my children but didn't want to impose on them and their families. So I would "eat my morsel alone." Sometimes I would go to a restaurant, sit, look at that empty seat across from me, then get up and leave to go home and eat my hot dog.

Many things were amusing. My girls would come by my office before every service and kiss me on the cheek. I thought that was so sweet of them until one day it dawned on me what they were doing.

Before they left the office they would say, "Dad, you're not going to wear that, are you?"

I would answer, "Well, I thought I would."

I kept clothes in a closet in my office, so they would go over and start looking through them, saying something like, "You probably have something that would look better." They would pick out another coat, shirt, or tie for me to wear, so I dressed well for every service.

I had friends seeking to introduce me to ladies, but I turned them all down. I dated no one. God spoke to me about JoAnn, and I knew that if He wanted me to marry again He would do the same again. He did not speak as He did before but impressed upon me greatly that Joan Carouthers was the one He wanted me to marry. So, the first week of January 2004, I called her. We were not strangers as I had met Joan and Kelton in 1955 before they were married. They married in 1957, and we became friends. They preached revivals for me in LaMarque and Pasadena. We preached for them when they settled down to pastor. They were in our home many times, and we would go to their special occasions. Kelton regarded me as his mentor. His children regarded me as their "second daddy." Whenever Karen would see me, she would run to me and throw up her arms for me to take her. After being Home Missions director for the Texas District for ten years, Kelton resigned and accepted the pastorate of the United Pentecostal Church in Jacksonville, Texas.

Me and Geri

Rich, me, JoAnn, Cathy, and Letha

Me and Joan

Before he accepted the position of Home Missions director, he pastored in Dallas. When he left Dallas, Rex Johnson accepted the church. After the tragic death of Brother Johnson's wife and son, he resigned, and Tom Foster was elected as pastor.

That church has become one of the great churches in Texas. Kelton's son, Mark Carouthers, graduated from Jackson College of Ministries and came to Pasadena as our music director. He was one of the best, and we worked together beautifully. He married Lori Lewis while with me, and I was privileged to assist Kelton in performing the ceremony. He was with us for six years, and then I reluctantly gave them up when they went to Indiana Bible College as music instructors. Kelton suffered a heart attack on June 11, 1998, and died. I lost one of my closest friends.

Six years after his death, I called Joan and invited her to Pasadena on Memorial Day weekend. She stayed with her close friends, Barclay and Norma Barnett, the father- and mother-in-law of Brother Kenneth Gurley. She came to church in Pasadena Sunday morning.

The next day I went to Rich's home, where they had a number of things that were mine. I wanted Cathy, Letha, and Rich to choose what they wanted to keep. After working a couple of hours, they surrounded me, had me sit on the floor as they did, and began questioning me. They said, "All right, Dad, what's going on with you and Joan?" I answered that we had dated a few times. They said, "Dad, we want you to marry her. We like her! She fits into our family just fine! So marry her just as soon as possible! You need her!"

What could I say? I told them that I would ask her and see what her answer would be. She had a birthday the next week, and I was invited to Arlington for her birthday party. When I arrived, a number were already there. After a few minutes, I asked her daughter, Karen, and Brian, Karen's husband, to come outside for a minute as I wanted to ask them something. I asked, "Karen, do you mind me asking your mother to marry me?"

Her answer was, "No! It would be wonderful!"

When Mark arrived, I pulled him aside and asked him the same question. His answer was the same as Karen's.

When it came time for the gifts to be opened, she got to mine last. I had a gift, a Movado watch and also a leather carry-on bag. She pushed the bag aside and reached for the other gift, and I said, "No, the other gift comes after you look at the bag."

She said, "I see it."

"Open it first," I said.

She opened the bag and took out a plaque that read, "Let us grow old together. The best is yet to come." She screamed and started to cry.

The others wanted to know what was happening until she showed them the plaque. After they saw the plaque, they all started crying. I didn't expect to cause such a scene!

Then she reached for the other gift, but I said, "No, it's not yours until you give me an answer!" That was her sixty-fifth birthday. Oh, by the way, she said, "Yes."

I went home and told my children, and the first thing they asked was, "When is the date?" I told them that no date was set.

They said, "We want it to be as soon as possible!"

I called Joan and told her what my children had said and added that I wanted it to be in two weeks, Father's Day. She said she couldn't make it that soon. She hung up and told Karen what I had said.

Karen said, "We'll make it by that date if that is what you both want." I guess she was afraid I would back out. You see, when you reach our ages, we must move fast. None of our children wanted to take care of us any longer. Let us take care of each other!

So the date was set for Sunday evening with the whole church invited. Our families were there. Geron and Becky couldn't make it, but Gerica was there and was a part of the wedding party. Rich, announcing the shower, stated, "They are registered at Walgreens."

I would like to say to anyone who is a preacher and has lost a mate that it is not wrong to marry again. I know Geri had mentioned to me that she did not want me to be alone. It is lonely! A preacher needs a wife. A church needs a "church mother." I would encourage you to stay in the ministry with whom you choose. Joan is absolutely wonderful! Her family is mine, and my family is hers. JoAnn's family blends in with us as well. They are still "my children." I am amazed that I have had three wonderful ladies who loved God with all their hearts and proved that they loved me in being so good to me. God blessed me with them! Maybe it was because I wouldn't make a move until I knew He was in it.

On my eightieth birthday, all my "children" helped me celebrate it. Geron and Becky Davis, Bryan and Karen Jenkins, Mark and Lori Carouthers, Todd and Letha Wise, Gary and Cathy Dennard, Rich and Kerri Glass were all there. It was a wonderful occasion, and the food was good, too.

My family

My son Rich loves to tease me, saying he has married me more times than I have married him. He was asked by the South Texas District to make a DVD that they may honor me at the District Convention. He took excerpts from sermons I had preached. I made the statement, "I said to my wife..." He took that statement and showed a picture of me with Geri; then repeated it again, "I said to my wife..."and showed a picture of me with JoAnn; then repeated it again, and showed a picture of me with Joan. You can imagine the laughs when they showed it to the conference. You can see from the picture that I now have quite a family, of whom I am extremely proud. He was announcing to the church about someone's fiftieth wedding anniversary, and I said to him, "Son, I have fifty years of marriage!" He asked what I meant, and I told him, "It has taken three wives for me to make fifty years, but I made it!"

I was greatly blessed when our general superintendent honored me by presenting to me at the General Conference in 2008 the plaque "Order of the Faith," making me a member of that elite group. But the greatest honor of all was when Jesus Christ made me His son! I John 3:1, "Behold what manner of love the Father hath bestowed upon us, that we should be called the sons of God!" That is the greatest blessing and honor of them all!

Kenneth Haney and Jerry Jones presenting me
the Order of Faith honor

My family at the banquet for
the Order of the Faith presentation

I am so thankful for all the rich blessings of the Lord Jesus Christ! I shudder to think what life would have been without Him. He has delivered me when there seemed no way. He has blessed me more than I can imagine. I have no regrets except I wish I would have started with Him at an earlier age. He's done me nothing but good! Today I love everybody; I have no enemies, only a great multitude of friends and a wonderful family.

Years ago my brother, George, had a minister approach him and wanted to tell him what his "enemies" were saying about him.

George answered, "I have no enemies!"

The man answered, "Oh, but you do, Brother Glass."

George continued, "If they feel I am an enemy to them, I would like to assure them that they are no enemy to me."

General Robert E. Lee was approached by another general who said, "What do you think of that officer?"

"I think he is a fine, outstanding officer and will be an asset to the United States army," Lee responded.

The General then said, "Then you don't know what he thinks of you!"

He answered, "You didn't ask me what he thought of me. I am saying what I think of him."

So now, having my eighty-third birthday, and much closer to Heaven, I will ride off into the sunset, having lived a rich, full, wonderful, and exciting life. If I can preach a few more sermons along the way, I will love it! It will continue to be Jesus all the way!

Gus Gustafson, who was like a blood brother; me; JoAnn; and Lorene, who was my wife's adopted sister

Joan and me with our strong help at headquarters,
Tom and Sue jackson

One of our greatest supporters and best friend,
James Lumpkin

The Milestones in My Life

ARLESS RICHEY GLASS

- Born to Robert Newton and Allie Glass on August 17, 1929, in DeRidder, Louisiana
- Graduated from DeRidder High School, class of 1947
- Began working at Crosby Chemical 1947, promoted to process chemist
- Entered the United States Air Force on September 27, 1950
- Served as welfare supervisor in the chaplaincy at Kadena AFB, Okinawa, July 1951 to June 1953
- Preached on Armed Forces Radio Network, 1952— Recorded and used every three months
- Missions work on Okinawa; baptized first person ever baptized there in Jesus' name in 1951
- Rotated to Carswell AFB, Texas, July 1953
- Married to Geraldine Gill of DeRidder, Louisiana, June 16, 1953
- Became parents of three children, Cathy, Letha, and Richey
- Blessed with six grandchildren
- Licensed as a minister in the United Pentecostal Church, February 1951—ordained July 1953

- Honorably discharged from the air force at Carswell AFB, October 16, 1953, as a staff sergeant
- Entered evangelistic work for UPCI, October 18, 1953, all over United States and Canada
- Assumed pastorate of the United Pentecostal Church, Lamarque, Texas, November 26, 1956, to August 1962
- Served as Sunday School director of Greater Houston Area, 1958-64
- Assumed the pastorate of the United Pentecostal Church, Pasadena, Texas, August 26, 1962, to present
- One of the founding fathers of Texas Bible College, January 1964
- Served as Foreign Missions director of Texas District, UPCI, 1965-70
- A teacher at Texas Bible College, January 1964-76
- Served on the Board of Directors of Texas Bible College, 1964-76
- Earned a Bachelor of Theology Degree, 1975
- A member of the Auxiliary United States Air Force, Civil Air Patrol, 1974-2006—Rank of Lt. Col.
- Appointed police chaplain for the Pasadena Police Department, Pasadena, TX, 1974 to present
- Appointed superintendent of education and chairman of Board of Education of UPCI, 1976-2006
- A member of National Conference on Ministries to the Armed Forces, 1977 to present
- Organized Summer Seminar of all UPCI Bible colleges in United States and Canada, 1978
- Appointed endorsing agent for the Military Chaplaincy of UPCI, March 1976 to present
- Fathered the Military Chaplain program for UPCI, 1977
- A member of Texas District Board of UPCI, 1992 to present
- A member of General Board, the ruling body of UPCI

- Elected to Board of Directors of Baptist Mortgage Trust, a lending institution, 1992-2002
- Received an Honorary Doctorate of Pentecostal Studies, 1991, from Apostolic Bible Institute, St. Paul, Minnesota
- One of the founding fathers of Urshan Graduate School of Theology, St. Louis, Missouri, 2001
- Traveled many times in overseas ministries and preached conferences, camp meetings, graduations, special services, and seminars throughout the world
- Received Masters Diploma for Apostolic Studies from World Academy of Letters, 2008
- After forty-two years of marriage, my wife Geraldine passed away.
- In 1996, married JoAnn Cannon, who was Ladies' Ministries President of Louisiana District, UPCI; she passed away 2002
- Presently married to Joan Carouthers of Arlington, Texas
- Listed in Who's Who in America and Who's Who of Executives and Professionals
- Presented the Order of the Faith award by the United Pentecostal Church International, 2008
- Appointed honorary member of the UPCI Board of Education, Board of Regents, General Board, and South Texas District Board
- Elected as bishop of the Pentecostals of Pasadena, Texas